BEST OF
Dublin

Oda O'Carroll

Best of Dublin
2nd edition – September 2004
First published – March 2002

Published by Lonely Planet Publications Pty Ltd
ABN 36 005 607 983

Australia	Head Office, Locked Bag 1, Footscray, Vic 3011
	☎ 03 8379 8000 fax 03 8379 8111
	🖳 talk2us@lonelyplanet.com.au
USA	150 Linden St, Oakland, CA 94607
	☎ 510 893 8555 toll free 800 275 8555
	fax 510 893 8572
	🖳 info@lonelyplanet.com
UK	72–82 Rosebery Avenue, London EC1R 4RW
	☎ 020 7841 9000 fax 020 7841 9001
	🖳 go@lonelyplanet.co.uk
France	1 rue du Dahomey, 75011 Paris
	☎ 01 55 25 33 00 fax 01 55 25 33 01
	🖳 bip@lonelyplanet.fr
	www.lonelyplanet.fr

This title was commissioned in Lonely Planet's London office and produced by: **Commissioning Editors** Amanda Canning, Alan Murphy **Coordinating Editors** Rebecca Lalor, Imogen Bannister **Coordinating Cartographers** Sarah Slone, Kusnandar **Layout Designer** Steven Cann **Proofer** Jackey Coyle **Cartographer** Joelene Kowalski **Managing Cartographer** Mark Griffiths **Cover Designers** Gerilyn Attebery, Wendy Wright **Project Manager** Eoin Dunlevy **Series Designer** Gerilyn Attebery **Mapping Development** Paul Piaia **Regional Publishing Manager** Amanda Canning **Thanks to** Ryan Evans, Corinne Waddell, Charles Rawlings-Way, Adriana Mammarella, Mark Germanchis, Darren O'Connell, Bruce Evans

Photographs by Lonely Planet Images, Olivier Cerindini and Jonathan Smith except for the following: p40 Eoin Clarke; p17, p24, p46, p48 Richard Cummins; p48, p50 Greg Gawlowski; p11, p24, p92 Doug McKinlay; p110 Emma Miller; p40, p99 Martin Moos; p11 Corey Wise; p46 Tony Wheeler. **Cover photograph** Merrion Square, Dublin, Ireland Scott Smith/Photolibrary.com. All images are copyright of the photographers unless otherwise indicated. Many of the images in this guide are available for licensing from Lonely Planet Images: 🖳 www.lonelyplanetimages.com.

ISBN 1 74059 490 8

Printed by Colorcraft Ltd, Hong Kong
Printed in China

Acknowledgements © Dublin Transit map Iarnród Éireann 2004

HOW TO USE THIS BOOK

Colour-Coding & Maps

Each chapter has a colour code along the banner at the top of the page which is also used for text and symbols on maps (eg, all venues reviewed in the Highlights chapter are orange on the maps). The fold-out maps inside the front and back covers are numbered from 1 to 6. All sights and venues in the text have map references; eg, (4, D7) means Map 4, grid reference D7. See p129 for map symbols.

Prices

Multiple prices listed with reviews (eg €10/5) usually indicate adult/concession admission to a venue. Concession prices can include senior, student, member or coupon discounts. Meal cost and room rate categories are listed at the start of the Eating and Sleeping chapters, respectively.

Text Symbols

☎	telephone
✉	address
🖳	email/website address
€	admission
☺	opening hours
ⓘ	information
🚆	train
🚈	light rail
🚌	bus
Ⓟ	parking available
♿	wheelchair access
✖	on-site/nearby eatery
☗	child-friendly venue
Ⓥ	good vegetarian selection

Contents

From the Publisher

AUTHOR

Oda O'Carroll

Coming from the lesser reaches of Roscommon in the mid-west, Oda remembers the excitement of childhood trips to Dublin in her mother's Renault 18, trawling through the Dandelion market in search of luminous nail varnish and the thrill of eating in fast-food joints (they hadn't yet hit her home town!). Almost two decades, one husband and two daughters later, she still loves it and was only too happy to revisit her secret haunts to give you the lowdown on the best city in the world.

Oda also works as a screenwriter and has contributed to LP's *Ireland, Britain, France* and *Corsica* titles.

Oda thanks James O'Neill and Freddy Daly in the Hugh Lane Gallery for the cracking unofficial tour, Amanda and Alan in LP's London office for their wisdom and wit, the luscious ladies who lunch Charlotte, Clare, Kate, Orla, Katell and Etain, and of course the ever-dependable Eoin and her little fairies, Ésa and Mella.

The 1st edition of this book was written by Emma Miller.

PHOTOGRAPHER

Olivier Cerindini

A journalist and photographer based in Paris, Olivier has contributed to the writing of many Lonely Planet guidebooks in the French language. Apart from pens and notebooks, his cameras have always been his most faithful travel companions. After years of black and white photography, he slowly allowed his world to become quadrichromatic and became a regular contributor to Lonely Planet Images.

Jonathan Smith

Raised in the Scottish Highlands, Jon found himself unsure of what to do after uni, so he took a flight to Vilnius and spent the next four years travelling around the former USSR. Having tried everything from teaching to translating Lithuanian cookbooks into English, Jon resolved to seek his fortune as a freelance travel photographer. Since then Jon's byline has appeared in 50 Lonely Planet titles, notably Edinburgh, Prague and Moscow.

Introducing Dublin

Riding the crest of a remarkable economic boom, Dublin's landscape has changed immeasurably over the past decade. The Irish Republic's capital and its heart, Dublin now ranks among the top tourist destinations in Europe.

Years of intense urban renewal have rejuvenated the once shady streets of the city centre, and many Dubliners have embraced this new sophistication with unadulterated glee. For the first time in its independent history, the city is strutting its stuff with unshakeable confidence.

Come to Dublin and you can't help but enjoy the energy, humour and relaxed attitude of its people. The city's many historic museums, top-class attractions and Georgian architecture aside, it's the genuine social interaction and legendary craic (traditional fun) that make the place magnetic.

Ireland's economic revival has now become the stuff of legend and while the Celtic Tiger's roar may have quietened in recent years, the unparalleled optimism and positivity felt by Dubliners is still evident all over the city. The attendant migration of people from all corners of the globe to Ireland, and particularly Dublin, has added a cosmopolitan and culturally diverse element to the city's personality. New hotels, restaurants, bars and cafés crop up almost daily and, on the surface at least, there appears to be a blissful ignorance of economic downturnings. What remains special about the city today – as it always has – is the spirit of the people, who ensure that despite whirlwind changes, Dublin remains one of Europe's most down-to-earth, friendly and accessible cities.

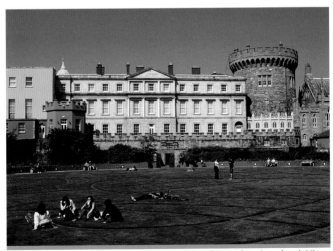

Take a well-earned break from sightseeing at the Chester Beatty Library's gardens (p14)

Neighbourhoods

Greater Dublin sprawls around Dublin Bay, bounded to the north by the Howth hills and to the south by the Dalkey headland with the river Liffey dividing the city. Dublin's main suburban train line, the Dublin Area Rapid Transit (DART), runs along the coast, linking the seaside suburbs with the city centre while a long-awaited light rail line, LUAS, connects southside suburbs with the centre. The rest of Dublin must rely on private cars, gridlocked buses, the limited Suburban Rail service, pedal or foot power.

Major transport hubs for inter-city travel are Connolly Station (4, F3) and Busáras bus terminal (4, E4) in the city's northeast, and Heuston Station (3, D3) on the southside.

Dublin's city centre lies between two semicircular arcs formed by the Grand Canal to the south and the Royal Canal to the north. The centre is compact and best seen on foot, though at times the footpaths are so crowded it seems the entire population of the capital is on the move.

South of the Liffey, the main promenade and the heart of town is pedestrianised **Grafton St**, where flower stalls, buskers, pavement artists and beggars compete to divert your gaze from the upmarket shops. The well-heeled streets **east of Grafton St** offer book, jewellery and craft shops and art galleries as well as gastronomic pubs and cafés for flush folk. The area around **Nassau St**, which borders the southern side of Trinity College (p9), is constantly awash with shops selling high-end, traditional Irish crafts and goods. The younger and funkier crowd lounge outside the cafés **west of Grafton St** where the tangle of streets offers offbeat clothing, gourmet delis, clubs and pubs. Dublin's own version of Chinatown is very small and basically comprises an Asian market and a handful of restaurants in the block around **Drury St**. Immediately south of here the aroma of espresso wafts from a little pocket

Off the Beaten Track

Dublin's city centre can get horribly congested with both people and cars, but it's not difficult to find some peace. For a real escape head to the seaside suburbs, or try these more central idylls:

- Iveagh Gardens (p35)
- Newman University Church (p33)
- The bookshop at the Hugh Lane Gallery (p61)
- The garden at the Chester Beatty Library (p14)
- The lakeside area at the National Botanic Gardens (p27)
- RHA Gallagher Gallery (p32)
- Grand Canal towpath (p35)

Iveagh Gardens offer peaceful shelter

of Italian eateries, pizzerias and food shops on **Chatham St** where Dublin's Italian community breaks bread. Heading north, on the far side of **Dame St** is **Temple Bar** (p16), one of Dublin's rowdiest, most alcohol-fuelled areas. Walk it during the day, though, and you'll find interesting galleries as well as funky record and design shops.

Out towards the Guinness Storehouse (p13) **the Liberties** is one of the city's oldest areas and an interesting place to stroll – try Thomas St, the antique district of Francis St and the old market area of Meath St. Across the river, the traffic artery of **O'Connell St** was laid waste in the 1916 Easter Rising and was extensively rebuilt last century. There are major make-over plans afoot, but for now it's sadly lined with cheap department stores and burger joints. Crossing O'Connell St, **Henry St** and **Talbot St** are lined with chain stores and discount outlets and buzz with people and street traders selling everything from cheap tobacco to football scarves. **Moore St** hosts an outdoor fruit and vegetable market (p60), a relic of the fast-disappearing 'auld' Dublin. West of here the ramshackle factories of **Smithfield** are slowly being converted into modern apartments, though big plans for its rejuvenation have never fully materialised.

To get a sense of how diverse Dublin is, catch the DART to the quiet, affluent **seaside suburbs** (p39) north and south of the centre, such as Dalkey and Howth.

Ain't nothing like a Dame, or like Dame St traffic on a Friday night

Itineraries

Dublin's main sights might not visually rival those of flashier European capitals, but they offer rich historical and literary tales for those who care to listen. Most of the major sights are south of the river Liffey and within easy walking distance of each other.

During summer, queues can be horrendous at popular attractions; arrive early. Most fee-paying sights offer discounts to students, the elderly, children and families. You can also get discounts by block-buying tickets for Dublin Tourism–administered sights. It's only worth getting the Heritage Card from the **Office of Public Works** (☎ 647 2453; www .heritageireland.ie; €20/7.50-15/50) if you're travelling around the rest of the country.

Dublin Lowlights
Some things we could do without:
- Overpriced pints
- Rampant bicycle thieves
- Crass, soulless 'theme' bars
- Early-closing pubs and clubs
- The rain, the rain, the rain

'That'll teach him to steal my bike'

DAY ONE
Start early at **Trinity College** (p9) then take a stroll in **St Stephen's Green** (p18). See the **National Museum** (p11, p21, p26) and **National Gallery** (p12) then mosey through **the Liberties** (p7) to the **Guinness Storehouse** (p13). Eat dinner at **L'Ecrivain** (p77) then retire to the **Stag's Head** (p87) for drinks.

DAY TWO
Start at the **Chester Beatty Library** (p14) in **Dublin Castle** (p20) then see **Christ Church Cathedral** (p15) and **Marsh's Library** (p25), before a spot of shopping around **Grafton St** (p53). Dine at **Trocadero** (p75) before seeing a play. Enjoy a nightcap at the **Palace Bar** (p87).

DAY THREE
Explore the northside with a walk along the Liffey **Boardwalk** (5, A2) and picnic at the **National Botanic Gardens** (p27) or take a DART to the **James Joyce Museum** (p17) at Sandycove. Alternatively, you could head west to the **Irish Museum of Modern Art** (p19) and **Kilmainham Gaol** (p22). Unwind with afternoon tea at the **Méridien Shelbourne Hotel** (p99), then dine at the **Mermaid Café** (p7).

Highlights

TRINITY COLLEGE (2)

Ireland's premier university is both a tranquil retreat from the bustle of the city, and the home of Dublin's biggest attraction, the Book of Kells.

Established by Elizabeth I in 1592 on land confiscated from an Augustinian priory, Trinity College was the queen's attempt to stop Irish youth from being 'infected with popery'.

The college remains one of Europe's best universities, with a legion of notable graduates. Until 1793 Trinity College remained completely Protestant. Even when the university began to admit Catholics, the Catholic Church forbade it – a restriction not completely lifted until 1970. Today most of its 13,000 students are Catholic.

Heading through the Regent House entrance on College Green, you come to a large square which is technically three separate squares, dominated by the 30m-high **Campanile** (2, B1). Designed by Edward Lanyon and erected in 1853, legend has it that students who cross beneath it when the bells toll will fail their exams.

On the east side of Library Sq, the red-brick **Rubrics building** (2, B1) dates from around 1690, making it the oldest building in the college, though it has been extensively altered.

The modernist **Berkeley Library** (2, B2) was designed in 1967 by Paul Koralek in the solid, square, brutalist style.

Most visitors to Trinity come to see the fabulous **Book of Kells**, an illuminated manuscript dating from around AD 800 and one of the oldest books in the world, housed in the **Old Library** (enter from Fellows' Sq; 2, B2; ☎ 608 2320). The Book of Kells was probably produced by monks at St Columba's Monastery on the remote Scottish island of Iona. It moved with the monks to Kells in County Meath in AD 806 after

INFORMATION

☎ 677 2941

✉ College Green

€ grounds free; Book of Kells €7.50/6.50/15, under 12 free

⌚ grounds 8am-midnight; Old Library/Book of Kells 9.30am-5pm Mon-Sat, to 4.30pm Sun, from noon Sun Oct-May

ⓘ 30min walking tours (☎ 608 1724; €9, incl entry to Book of Kells) from 10.15am every 40min from Front Sq Jun-Sep

🚇 Pearse Station, Tara St

♿ good

🍽 Buttery Café & Bar, cafeteria in Arts & Social Science Bldg

The Long Room has a long list of books

repeated Viking raids and was brought to Trinity College for safekeeping in 1654.

The manuscript contains the four New Testament gospels written in Latin, as well as prefaces, summaries and other text. The superbly decorated lettering and the complex, intertwining illustrations are impressive. Admission to the Book of Kells includes the 65m-long **Library Long Room**, which contains 200,000 ancient books and manuscripts. A rare copy of the **Proclamation of the Irish Republic**, read by Patrick Pearse at the beginning of the 1916 Easter Rising, is also here.

South across Fellows' Sq is the **Arts & Social Science building** (2, B2), also designed by Paul Koralek and home to the **Douglas Hyde Gallery** (p31). **Dublin Experience** (2, B2; ☎ 608 1688; €4.20/3.50/9; hourly, 10am-5pm mid-May–Sep) provides a 45-minute audiovisual introduction to the city.

Trinity Scholars

Famous alumni of Trinity College include politicians Edmund Burke, Wolfe Tone and Douglas Hyde and writers Jonathan Swift, Oliver Goldsmith, Samuel Beckett, Bram Stoker and Oscar Wilde. More recent graduates include former president Mary Robinson and her successor, Mary McAleese, both of whom studied law.

Women were first admitted to the college in 1903, but only after a bitter battle with George Salmon, the college's provost from 1886 to 1904. Salmon, whose statue (2, B1) stands just north of the Campanile, famously carried out his threat to permit women 'over his dead body' by dropping dead when the worst happened.

George Salmon, now condemned to watch the college's female students walk by every day

NATIONAL MUSEUM OF IRELAND – ARCHAEOLOGY & HISTORY (6, F3)

The National Museum is home to a fabulous bounty of Bronze Age gold, Iron Age Celtic metalwork, Viking artefacts and some impressive ancient Egyptian relics. The Victorian Palladian-style building is a fine setting for the collection, with its 18.9m domed rotunda, classical marble columns and mosaic floors.

The exhibition begins in **Prehistoric Ireland**, with Stone Age burial mounds and Bronze Age tools, spearheads and domestic objects. An early Iron Age **bog body**, its leathery skin gruesomely preserved, is sure to impress kids.

There is an exceptional amount of Bronze Age Irish gold, much of it unearthed from bogs by farmers' ploughs or peat-cutters' saws, on show in **Ór – Ireland's Gold**. The stunning jewellery, dating from 7000–2000 BC, ranges from simple lunulae – sun discs and crescents – to elaborate bracelets, earrings and neckpieces.

Two of the museum's best pieces are in the **Treasury**. The **Ardagh Chalice**, found by a farmer in 1868, is made of 354 pieces of precious metal and considered the finest example of Celtic art ever found. Also here is the **Tara Brooch**, intricately decorated with filigree gold wire, enamelled studs, amber bands and amethysts.

INFORMATION

- ☎ 677 7444
- 🖳 www.museum.ie
- ✉ Kildare St
- € free
- 🕙 10am-5pm Tue-Sat, 2-5pm Sun
- ℹ regular guided tours €2, family programmes at weekends (call ahead)
- 🚌 7, 7a, 10, 25X, 39X, 51D, 51X
- 🚉 Pearse Station
- ♿ limited
- ✕ on-site museum restaurant

DON'T MISS

- Broighter Hoard
- Cross of Cong
- Lurgan Logboat
- *Ten Years Collecting* exhibit

The National Museum of Ireland, fabulous finds for the oldies, gruesome bodies for the kids

NATIONAL GALLERY OF IRELAND (4, E7)

The National Gallery opened in 1864 and has built up a sizable collection of Irish, British and European art. Its original collection of 125 paintings has grown, mainly through bequests, to around 12,500 artworks, including oils, watercolours, drawings, prints and sculptures.

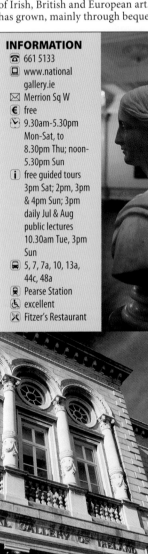

INFORMATION

- ☎ 661 5133
- 🖥 www.national gallery.ie
- ✉ Merrion Sq W
- € free
- 🕑 9.30am-5.30pm Mon-Sat, to 8.30pm Thu; noon-5.30pm Sun
- ⓘ free guided tours 3pm Sat; 2pm, 3pm & 4pm Sun; 3pm daily Jul & Aug public lectures 10.30am Tue, 3pm Sun
- 🚌 5, 7, 7a, 10, 13a, 44c, 48a
- 🚉 Pearse Station
- ♿ excellent
- 🍴 Fitzer's Restaurant

Treasures await within

On the ground floor is the glittering **Shaw Room**, named after playwright George Bernard Shaw, who was a major gallery benefactor. The room, with its full-length portraits, busts and Waterford-crystal chandeliers, hosts weekend summer concerts.

The **Yeats Museum** displays paintings by Jack B Yeats (1871–1957), his father, the noted portraitist John B Yeats (1839–1907), and sisters Anne and Lily. The ground-floor **Milltown Wing** houses Irish art, while the **North Wing** has Irish portraiture, big-name Brits such as Gainsborough and Turner, the **Print Gallery** which holds changing exhibitions, and the **Spanish collection**, with works by El Greco, Goya, Velázquez and Picasso.

On the upper levels, periods covered include Italian Early Renaissance to 18th century and French 17th to 19th centuries. A highlight is Caravaggio's *The Taking of Christ,* which lay undiscovered for more than 60 years in a Jesuit house in Leeson St until spotted by the chief curator of the gallery, Sergio Benedetti, in 1990.

The bright, ultramodern **Millennium Wing** on Clare St has two floors of galleries for visiting exhibitions, a multimedia room and a centre for the study of Irish art. The gallery also has excellent kids' programmes on Saturdays that run almost daily in summer.

DON'T MISS

- Jack B Yeats' *The Liffey Swim*
- Vermeer's *Lady Writing a Letter*
- Gainsborough's *The Cottage Girl*
- Picasso's *Still Life with Mandolin*

GUINNESS STOREHOUSE (3, D4)

Like Disneyland for beer lovers, the Guinness Storehouse is an all-singing, all-dancing extravaganza combining sophisticated exhibits with more than a pintful of marketing.

Housed in an old grain storehouse opposite the original **St James's Gate Brewery**, the Storehouse is an impressive enterprise that uses high-tech multimedia displays to tell the story of Guinness.

Founded by Arthur Guinness in 1759, St James's Gate brews an astounding 450 million litres of Guinness a year, exporting to 150 countries.

Exhibits in the €38-million centre are spread over five storeys. On the ground floor you enter the **Experience** and see how water, barley, hops and yeast combine to create the world-famous stout.

Cooperage is one of the simplest and most informative exhibits, showing how highly skilled coopers once hammered each and every cask into shape. In **Advertising** you can replay your favourite Guinness ads then pop downstairs to the superstore and buy yourself a monogrammed tie.

INFORMATION
- ☎ 408 4800
- 🖳 www.guinness-storehouse.com
- ✉ St James's Gate
- € €13.50/5-9/30, under 6 free
- 🕑 9.30am-9pm Jul & Aug, 9.30am-5pm Sep-Jun
- 🚌 51b, 78a, 123
- 🚉 James's
- ♿ excellent
- 🍽 Brewery Bar

Like the creamy head on a pint of Guinness, though, the circular, rooftop **Gravity Bar** where you get your free glass of Guinness is the best part.

Working for Yer Man

In the 1930s when there were more than 5000 people working at St James's Gate, Guinness was the largest employer in the city. For nearly two centuries it was also one of the best places to work, paying 20% more than the minimum wage. Today, automation has reduced the workforce to around 600.

Water is only for making fountains and beer at the Guinness Storehouse

CHESTER BEATTY LIBRARY (6, A2)

The astounding collection of New York mining magnate Sir Alfred Chester Beatty (1875–1968) is the basis for one of Dublin's best, if less-visited, museums, winner of the prestigious Europe Museum of the Year in 2002. An avid traveller and collector from an early age, Beatty amassed more than 20,000 manuscripts and *objets d'art*. Beatty, who bequeathed the collection to the state, became Ireland's first honorary citizen in 1957 and the museum is testament to his exquisite taste and eye for intricate beauty.

INFORMATION

- ☎ 407 0750
- 🖥 www.cbl.ie
- ✉ Dublin Castle, Ship St
- € free
- 🕑 10am-5pm Mon-Fri, 11am-5pm Sat, 1-5pm Sun; closed Mon Oct-Apr
- ℹ free tours 1pm Wed, 3pm & 4pm Sun; monthly kids workshops
- 🚌 50, 51b, 77, 78a, 123
- ♿ good
- ✕ Silk Road Café

The 1st-floor gallery begins with memorabilia from Beatty's life, before embarking on an exploration of the art of Mughal India, Persia, the Ottoman Empire, Japan and China.

The library's 2nd floor is devoted to major world religions. Head for the collection of Korans from the 9th to the 19th centuries, considered to be among the best illuminated Islamic texts. You'll also find ancient Egyptian papyrus texts and exquisite artwork from Burma, Indonesia and Tibet.

DON'T MISS

- Japanese samurai armour
- Qing dynasty dragon Robe
- 17th-century snuff bottles
- Landscaped roof garden

Chester Beatty collected manuscripts, *objets d'art* and lego

CHRIST CHURCH CATHEDRAL (4, B6)

Dublin's most imposing church, Christ Church Cathedral, lies within the city's original Norse settlement and the old heart of medieval Dublin. It has been the state Church of Ireland since its inception.

Built on the site of an existing wooden Viking church, the stone cathedral was commissioned in 1172 by the Anglo-Norman conqueror of Dublin, Richard de Clare ('Strongbow'), and Archbishop Laurence O'Toole.

The cathedral was restored several times over the centuries, resulting in architectural styles that range from Romanesque to Gothic. Much of the building now dates from 1871–78, when the cathedral was rescued from ruin by a £230,000 donation (€30 million in today's terms) from whiskey distiller Henry Roe. The north wall, transepts and western part of the choir remain from the original.

Highlights include the **Chapel of St Laud**, which contains the embalmed heart of Archbishop O'Toole and curiosities such as a mummified cat and rat.

The arched crypt, the oldest structure in Dublin, contains the **Treasury exhibit**, with rare coins, the Stuart coat of arms and gold given to the church by William of Orange after his victory at the Battle of the Boyne. It also shows how the Vikings built the original cathedral.

Try to visit just before **choral evensong** to catch the choir's wonderfully evocative recitals bringing the cathedral's rich atmosphere to life.

INFORMATION

- ☎ 677 8099
- 🖳 www.cccdub.ie
- ✉ Christ Church Pl
- € €5/2.50/7
- 🕐 9.45am-5pm Mon-Fri, 10am-5pm Sat & Sun
- ℹ choral evensong 5pm Thu & Sat, 3.30pm Sun; bell-ringing 7-9pm Fri (practice), 10-11am & 2.30-3.30pm Sun, New Year's Eve
- 🚌 50, 66, 77, 121, 123
- ✗ Queen of Tarts (p71)

The Bells, the Bells

The melodic sound of Christ Church's bells has been ringing through Dublin air since 1670. Nineteen bells, the greatest number rung in this way worldwide and weighing up to 2¼ tons each, are hand rung in a mathematical sequence, with training taking years to complete.

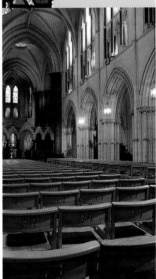

Built by faith, restored by whiskey

TEMPLE BAR (5)

It's tacky. It's touristy. It's packed with falling-down-drunks at night and carpeted with vomit of a morning but Temple Bar, the city's prime entertainment and eating spot, still has a certain something.

As one of Dublin's oldest areas, Temple Bar's fortunes have ebbed and flowed for centuries. The western boundary, **Fishamble St** (6, A1), is the city's oldest street, and dates to Viking times. Crime and prostitution moved in during the 18th century, followed by small craft and trade businesses in the 19th century.

INFORMATION

☎ 671 5717

🖥 www.templebar.ie

ℹ Temple Bar Properties has a walk-in info centre (12 Essex St E; 5, B2) on Temple Bar

🚌 all city-centre buses

🍴 see p69

Touristy maybe, but there's plenty of beer

By the first half of the 20th century Temple Bar had sunk into decline, along with most of central Dublin. A 1960s plan to build a major bus depot here was put on hold and by the 1980s the dilapidated area was home to a thriving community of artists and cultural groups who paid low or no rents. The government soon recognised that local energy, and in 1991 began a major revamp.

Ironically, among the tourist-fodder restaurants and pubs, you'll find some excellent galleries, off-beat shops and an independent cinema.

On Saturday Dublin's foodies, families and city strollers amass at the excellent **organic food market** in Meeting House Sq to sample everything from tapas and farmhouse cheeses, to oysters and Guinness.

By night from May to September the square transforms into an open-air cinema, sometimes accompanied by live music from the Ark's (p42) outdoor stage, as part of the annual **Diversions festival**.

Handel with Care

In 1742 the nearly broke GF Handel conducted the very first performance of his epic work *Messiah* in the since-demolished Dublin Music Hall, on the city's oldest street, Fishamble St (6, A1). Ironically, Dean Swift – author of *Gulliver's Travels* and dean of St Patrick's Cathedral – having suggested his own and Christchurch's choir participate, revoked his invitation, vowing to 'punish such vicars for their rebellion, disobedience and perfidy'. The concert went ahead nonetheless, and the celebrated work is now performed in Dublin annually.

JAMES JOYCE MUSEUM (1, C2)

Housed in a Martello tower overlooking Dublin Bay, the James Joyce Museum combines memorabilia from the celebrated writer's life with a dramatic setting that has a story all its own. The ground-floor museum has several 1st-edition Joyce books, as well as photographs, letters and one of two plaster death masks. Other items include an edition of *Ulysses* illustrated by Henri Matisse, Joyce's guitar and hunting vest and a page of original manuscript from *Finnegans Wake*.

The opening scene of *Ulysses* is set on the tower's roof. The tower was one of 26 built along the Dublin coast to defend against a threatened invasion by Napoleon.

Winding steps lead up to the **Round Room** where the 22-year-old Joyce stayed for a few days in September 1904. He was the guest of poet Oliver St John Gogarty, caricatured in *Ulysses* as the 'stately, plump Buck Mulligan'.

Just below the Martello tower is the **Forty Foot Pool**. At the close of the first chapter of *Ulysses*, Buck Mulligan heads to the pool for a morning swim, an activity which is still a local tradition. For years the spot was reserved for male-only nude bathing, but women are now allowed. Though a sign warns that 'togs must be worn', die-hard men still keep the tradition up before 9am.

INFORMATION

- ☎ 280 9265
- ✉ Martello tower, Sandycove, Co Dublin
- € €6.25/3.75-5.25/ 17.50
- ☼ 10am-1pm & 2-5pm Mon-Sat, 2-6pm Sun & hols Apr-Oct; by arrangement only Nov-Mar
- ⓘ open 8am-6pm Bloomsday (16 Jun) with special events
- 🚌 59 from Dun Laoghaire
- 🚉 Sandycove & Glasthule
- ♿ limited
- ✂ Caviston's (p80)

The Round Room Incident

By the time Joyce arrived to stay at the tower, Gogarty was somewhat less than happy to see him, having been branded a snob in Joyce's latest poem, 'The Holy Office'. One night, Gogarty's other guest, Samuel Trench (Haines in *Ulysses*), had a nightmare about a panther and, half asleep, fired a shot at the fireplace. Gogarty took the gun from him, yelled 'Leave him to me' and shot down the saucepans on the shelf above Joyce's bed. Joyce took the hint and left the next morning.

The spot to hunt panthers and skinny dip

ST STEPHEN'S GREEN   (4, D7)

Once a common where public whippings, burnings and hangings took place, the nine hectares of St Stephen's Green now provide a popular lunch-time escape for city workers. Geese, ducks and waterfowl splash about the ponds, there's a good children's playground and the bandstand hosts concerts in summer.

INFORMATION

- € free
- ☼ 8am-dusk Mon-Sat, from 10am Sun
- ⓘ Garden for the Blind has Braille signs and plants that can be handled
- 🚆 Pearse Station
- 🚉 St Stephen's Green
- ♿ good
- ✗ Bang Café (p77)

The fine Georgian buildings around the square date mainly from Dublin's 18th-century boom. Today the grand **Shelbourne Hotel** (p99) remains a popular society meeting place. A few doors along is a small **Huguenot Cemetery** (4, E7), established in 1693 for French Protestant refugees. The south side is home to beautifully restored **Newman House** (p38) and the Byzantine-inspired **Newman University Church** (p33).

Statues and **memorials** dot the green, including those of Sir Arthur Guinness and James Joyce. Around the central fountain are busts of Countess Markievicz and a 1967 Henry Moore sculpture of WB Yeats.

Surgeons' Seizure

During the 1916 Easter Rising, a band of Irish rebel forces occupied St Stephen's Green. They were led by Countess Constance Markievicz, the colourful Irish nationalist, and later the first woman elected to the Irish Parliament. Though Markievicz, who was married to a Polish count, failed to take the Shelbourne Hotel, the rebels seized the Royal College of Surgeons building on the western side of the square. If you look closely at its columns you can still see the bullet marks.

The pleasant side of all that rain; lush green trees and full ponds at St Stephen's Green

IRISH MUSEUM OF MODERN ART (3, C4)

The country's foremost gallery for contemporary art, the Irish Museum of Modern Art (IMMA) is spectacularly housed in the former **Royal Hospital Kilmainham**, once home to veteran soldiers.

Built between 1680 and 1684, the site languished for much of the 20th century until it was extensively restored and reopened as an art museum in 1991. The museum juxtaposes the work of major established artists with that of young up-and-comers.

The gallery's 4000-strong collection includes works by artists such as Picasso, Miró and Vasarely, as well as works by more contemporary artists including Gilbert and George, Gillian Wearing and Damien Hirst. The gallery displays ever-changing shows from its own works, and hosts regular touring exhibitions.

Modern Irish art is always on display and Irish and international artists live and work on site in the **converted coach houses** behind the south wing. The **New Galleries**, in the restored Deputy Master's House, should also not be missed.

While the art is often top-notch, it is the building that wows most visitors. With its striking classical facade and large central courtyard inspired by Les Invalides in Paris, the Royal Hospital is felt to be the city's finest surviving 17th-century building.

The museum is surrounded by lush green grounds and is bordered on the north side by a perfectly laid out **Formal Garden**, which has views across the river Liffey to Phoenix Park (p28).

INFORMATION

☎ 612 9900
🖥 www.modernart.ie
✉ Military Rd, Kilmainham
€ free
🕙 10am-5.30pm Tue-Sat, from noon Sun & hols
ℹ free exhibition tours 2.30pm Wed, Fri & Sun
🚌 26, 51, 78a, 79, 90, 123
♿ good
🍴 on-site café

Impressive building, impressive art

IMMA's Hidden Treasures

Guided Heritage Tours of the museum are worth taking to see parts of the building normally closed to the public. Highlights include the **banqueting hall**, lined with portraits of 22 monarchs and viceroys, and the **chapel**, which has an elaborate baroque ceiling and a set of Queen Anne gates. Tours run from June to September; call the museum for details.

DUBLIN CASTLE (6, A1)

The stronghold of British power in Ireland for 700 years, Dublin Castle is principally an 18th-century creation built on Norman and Viking foundations. Of the 13th-century Anglo-Norman fortress built on the site, only the record tower remains. The most fascinating part of the castle is underground – a chunk of the old city walls and moat.

Once the official residence of the British viceroys in Ireland and now used by the Irish Government, access is by tour only. Tours include **drawing rooms** with their beautiful plasterwork, once used as bedrooms by visitors to the castle. The castle **gardens** end in a high wall said to have been built for Queen Victoria's visit to block the sight of the Stephen St slums.

The **Throne Room**'s large gold throne is said to have been presented to the castle by William of Orange on winning the Battle of Boyne. The room's centrepiece, the decorative **Act of Union chandelier**, weighs more than a tonne.

The 25m-long **St Patrick's Hall** is where Irish presidents are inaugurated and is also used for state receptions. In the Lower Yard is the **Chapel Royal**, built in Gothic style by Francis Johnston from 1807 to 1814. The interior is wildly exuberant, while the exterior is decorated with the carved heads of Irish notables and saints.

INFORMATION

- ☎ 677 7129
- 🖳 www.dublin castle.ie
- ✉ Cork Hill, Dame St
- € €4/1.50-3
- 🕑 10am-5pm Mon-Fri, from 2pm Sat, Sun & hols
- ⓘ tours run every 30min; State Apartments can be closed at short notice, call ahead to check
- 🚌 50, 54, 56a, 77, 77a
- ♿ limited
- ✗ on-site café

Justice for all?

The **Figure of Justice** that faces the castle's Upper Yard from the Cork Hill entrance has a controversial history. The statue was seen as a snub by many Dubliners, who felt Justice was symbolically turning her back on the city. If that wasn't enough, when it rained the scales would fill with water and tilt, rather than remaining perfectly balanced. Eventually a hole was drilled in the bottom of each pan, restoring balance, of sorts.

Make time to visit the Dublin Castle

NATIONAL MUSEUM OF IRELAND –
DECORATIVE ARTS & HISTORY (3, D3)

Until it was decommissioned just over a decade ago, Collins Barracks, built in 1704 on the orders of Queen Anne, was the largest military barracks in the world. In 1997 the early neoclassical grey stone building on the Liffey's northern bank was given a sparkling, modern makeover and now houses the Decorative Arts & History collection of the National Museum of Ireland.

Inside the imposing exterior lies a treasure trove of artefacts ranging from silver, ceramics and glassware to weaponry, furniture and folk-life displays. Some of the best pieces are gathered in the *Curator's Choice* exhibition.

On the 1st floor is the museum's **Irish silver collection**, on the 2nd floor you'll find **Irish period furniture**, while the 3rd floor has simple and sturdy **Irish country furniture**. Modern furniture and design lovers will enjoy the exhibition on iconic Irish designer Eileen Gray (1878–1976), one of the museum's highlights. The fascinating *Way We Wore* exhibit displays Irish clothing and jewellery from the past 250 years. The exhibit highlights the symbolism jewellery had in bestowing messages of mourning, love and learning.

INFORMATION
- ☎ 677 7444
- 🖳 www.museum.ie
- ✉ Benburb St
- € free
- 🕑 10am–5pm Tue-Sat, from 2pm Sun
- ℹ special events & educational workshops for kids held regularly, free daily tours
- 🚌 25, 25a, 66, 67, 90
- 🚏 Museum
- ♿ excellent
- 🍴 Brambles Cafe

DON'T MISS
- Fonthill vase
- Lord Chancellor's mace
- Domville doll's house
- Eugene Rousseau's carp vase

Quick march to the former Collins Barracks, now home to the decorative arts

KILMAINHAM GAOL (3, C4)

One of Dublin's most sobering sights, Kilmainham Gaol oozes centuries of pain, oppression and suffering from its decrepit limestone hulk. Scene of countless emotional episodes along Ireland's rocky road to independence, the jail was home to many of the country's political heroes, martyrs and villains. Opened in 1796, Kilmainham Gaol saw thousands of prisoners pass through its corridors, including Robert Emmet and Countess Markievicz.

INFORMATION

- ☎ 453 5984
- 🖳 www.heritage ireland.ie
- ✉ Inchicore Rd, Kilmainham
- € €5/2-3.50/11
- ◷ 9.30am-6pm Apr-Sep; to 5.30pm Mon-Fri, 10am-6pm Sun Oct-Mar
- ⓘ last admission 90min before closing, admission by 90min tour only
- 🚌 51b, 78a, 79 from Aston Quay
- ♿ limited, call ahead
- ✖ on-site tearoom

The **East Wing**, modelled on London's Pentonville Prison, with metal catwalks suspended around a light-filled, vaulted room, allowed guards full view of all the cells. Graffiti, scratched and scrawled by prisoners in the cells, is moving stuff.

Kilmainham was left to ruin until the 1960s, when a team of volunteers set about the massive task of restoration.

Visits to Kilmainham include an excellent **museum**, the **prison chapel**, the exercise and execution yards and the dark, dank old wing. During the Great Famine, thousands of the poor, petty thieves and children were crammed in here.

The Uprising Executions

After the 1916 Easter Rising, 14 of the 15 rebel executions took place at Kilmainham. James Connolly, who was so badly injured during fighting he couldn't stand, was strapped to a chair to face the firing squad. The ruthlessness of the killings outraged the public, both in Ireland and England, and boosted the nationalist cause.

Another great place to take the kids; tell them to behave themselves or you'll lock them in

ST PATRICK'S CATHEDRAL (4, B7)

St Patrick himself is said to have baptised converts at a well within the cathedral grounds, so the cathedral stands on one of the earliest Christian sites in the city.

Although a church stood on the site from the 5th century, the present building, with several major alterations, dates from 1191.

A series of natural disasters plagued the cathedral in the 14th century, including a storm that collapsed the spire and a fire that destroyed the original bell tower. The religious turmoil of the 16th century also took its toll. When Henry VIII dissolved the monasteries in 1537, St Patrick's was ordered to hand over all of its estates, revenues and possessions and it was demoted to the rank of parish church.

Oliver Cromwell, during his 1649 visit to Ireland, converted St Patrick's to a stable for his army's horses. In 1666 the Lady Chapel was given to the newly arrived Hugenots, in whose hands it remained until 1816. Although the church's most famous dean, writer Jonathan Swift, did his utmost to preserve the building, by the end of the 18th century it was close to collapse. Salvation came from the Guinness family, who funded a major restoration in 1864.

Just inside the main entrance is **Swift's grave**, and that of his long-term companion, Esther Johnston, or Stella. The **monument** to Sir Benjamin Guinness' daughter is a tribute to the family's role in the cathedral's restoration. Fittingly, it stands beneath a window that bears the words 'I was thirsty and ye gave me drink'.

INFORMATION

- ☎ 453 9472
- 🖥 www.stpatricks cathedral.ie
- ✉ St Patrick's Close
- € €4.20/3.20/9.50
- 🕑 9am-5pm Mon-Fri, to 5.30pm Sat, 9-11am, 12.30-2.45pm & 4.30-5.30pm Sun Mar-Oct; 9am-5pm Mon-Sat, 9-11am & 12.30-3pm Sun Nov-Feb
- ℹ entry for worshippers only during services
- 🚌 49, 50, 54a, 56a, 77
- ♿ by prior arrangement
- ✖ Queen of Tarts (p71)

DON'T MISS

- The organ
- Celtic grave slabs
- Chapter House door
- Living Stones exhibition

Give thanks for Guinness

DUBLIN CITY GALLERY – THE HUGH LANE   (4, C3)

Housed in a spacious 18th-century townhouse designed by Sir William Chambers, the Hugh Lane gallery's fine collection bridges the gap between the National Gallery's (p12) old masters and the cutting-edge works on show at the Irish Museum of Modern Art (p19).

All the big names of French Impressionism and early-20th-century Irish art are here. Sculptures by Rodin and Degas, and paintings by Corot, Courbet, Manet and Monet sit alongside works by Jack B Yeats, William Leech and Nathaniel Hone.

The gallery's newest exhibit, **Francis Bacon Studio**, was painstakingly moved, in all its shambolic mess, from 7 Reece Mews, South Kensington, London, where the Dublin-born artist lived for 31 years. Bacon, who famously hated Ireland, would no doubt have found it amusing that a team of conservators spent years cataloguing scraps of newspaper, horse whips, old socks, dirty rags and dried-up paint and mouse droppings, to reverently reassemble it all in Dublin.

The gallery was founded in 1908 by wealthy art dealer Sir Hugh Lane, who died on the *Lusitania* in 1915, when the the ship was torpedoed by a German U-boat. A bitter row erupted between the National Gallery in London and the Hugh Lane Gallery over the jewels of his collection. Today, after years of wrangling, half the works are displayed in Dublin and half in London, on a rotating basis.

One of the best times to visit the gallery is on a Sunday when classical concerts are held in the sculpture hall. Call for details.

INFORMATION

- ☎ 874 1903
- 🖥 www.hughlane.ie
- ✉ Charlemont House, Parnell Sq N
- € gallery free Francis Bacon Studio €7/3.50, under 12 free; €3.50 for all 9.30am-noon Tue
- 🕐 9.30am-6pm Tue-Thu, to 5pm Fri-Sat, 11am-5pm Sun
- ℹ kids weekend workshops, concerts noon most Suns
- 🚌 3, 10, 16, 19, 123
- 🚉 Connolly Station
- ♿ limited
- 🍴 on-site café

Step up to some great art

DON'T MISS

- • Manet's *Eva Gonzales*
- • Renoir's *Parapluies*
- • Kathy Prendergast's *Waiting*
- • Walter Osborne's *Tea in the Garden*

MARSH'S LIBRARY (4, B7)

Virtually unchanged for 300 years, Marsh's Library is a glorious example of an 18th-century scholar's den. The beautiful, dark, oak bookcases, each topped with elaborately carved and gilded gables, are filled with some 25,000 books dating from the 15th to the early 18th century.

Founded in 1701 by Archbishop Narcissus Marsh (1638–1713), it is the oldest public library in Ireland and its collection includes maps and incunabula, or books printed before 1501. In its one nod to the 21st century, the library's current 'Keeper', Dr Muriel McCarthy, is the first woman to hold the post.

INFORMATION

- ☎ 454 3511
- 🖳 www.marsh library.ie
- ✉ St Patrick's Close
- € €2.50/1.50
- 🕐 10am-1pm & 2-5pm Mon & Wed-Fri, 10.30am-1pm Sat
- 🚌 50, 50a, 54, 54a, 56a
- ✕ Queen of Tarts (p71)

Apart from theological books and Bibles in dozens of languages, there are tomes on medicine, law, travel, literature, science, music and mathematics. The oldest, and one of the most beautiful, books in the library is Cicero's *Letters to his Friends*, printed in Milan in 1472.

The **Delmas Conservation Bindery**, which repairs and restores rare books, manuscripts, drawings and maps, operates from the library and it makes an appearance in *Ulysses*.

Swift Ambitions

Several items of the master satirist Jonathan Swift are kept in the library, including his copy of *History of the Great Rebellion*. His margin notes include a number of disparaging comments about Scots, of whom he seemed to have a low opinion.

You'll find a craicing good read at Marsh's Library

NATIONAL MUSEUM OF IRELAND – NATURAL HISTORY (6, F3)

Entering this museum is like stepping back in time to the year 1857. Scarcely changed since then, when Scottish explorer Dr David Livingstone delivered the inaugural lecture, this terrifically antiquated place eschews the 21st-century unashamedly. You won't find any multimedia touch-screen displays here but you can bet that younger (and many older) visitors will revel in the dusty dinosaur-era displays and authentic Victorian atmosphere.

INFORMATION

- ☎ 677 7444
- 🖳 www.museum.ie
- ✉ Merrion St
- € free
- 🕙 10am-5pm Tue-Sat, from 2pm Sun
- 🚌 7, 7a
- ♿ limited
- 🍴 Ely (p77)

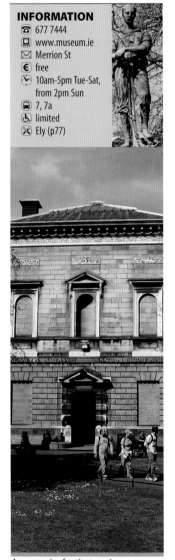

A menagerie of extinct species

The creaking interior gives way to an overwhelming display of stuffed animals and mounted heads, crammed in like something from a Hitchcock movie. Of the two million species on display in the museum, many are long extinct.

On the ground floor the **Irish Room** features a sizable collection of mammals, birds and butterflies, including three skeletons of giant Irish elk, a species that has been extinct for about 10,000 years. Suspended from the ceiling is a large basking shark, while some rather intriguing jars below contain parasites found in cats, dogs, pigs and sheep.

The **World Animals** collection, spread across the upper three levels, has as its centrepiece a 20m-long skeleton of a fin whale caught in Bantry Bay, County Cork. Other notables include a Tasmanian tiger (mislabelled as a Tasmanian wolf) and several African and Asian rhinoceroses.

Evolutionists will love the line-up of orang-utan, chimpanzee, gorilla and human skeletons housed in a glass cabinet on the 1st floor.

DON'T MISS

- Giant sunfish
- Great Irish wolfhound
- Dodo skeleton

GLASNEVIN (3, E1)

The northern suburb of Glasnevin is worth a visit for two adjoining historic sights. The **National Botanic Gardens** has been an important centre of horticultural and botanical study for more than 200 years. The Gardens' achievements include the first successful raising of orchids from seed (1844) and the introduction of pampas grass and lilies to the lawns of Europe. The highlight is a series of spectacular curvilinear **glasshouses** built from 1843 to 1869. Within are cacti, orchids and other exotic plants. In summer, don't miss the **giant Amazon water lily** in the Victoria House.

South is **Prospect Cemetery**, Ireland's largest cemetery and setting for part of *Ulysses*. It was established in 1832 for Roman Catholics. Many of the monuments are overtly patriotic, adorned with national symbols. The oldest section, near Prospect Sq, is the most interesting. The watchtowers built into the walls were once used to watch for body snatchers working for the city's 19th-century surgeons.

INFORMATION

- ☎ gardens 837 4388, cemetery 830 1133
- 💻 www.heritage ireland.ie, www.glasnevin-cemetery.ie
- ✉ enter gardens from Botanic Ave, cemetery from Finglas Rd
- € free
- 🕙 gardens 9am-6pm Apr-Oct, 10am-4.30pm Nov-Mar; cemetery 8am-5pm Mon-Sat
- ℹ free garden tours 2.30pm Sun from visitor centre (☎ 857 0909); free cemetery tours 2.30pm Wed & Fri
- 🚌 gardens 13, 19, 83; cemetery 40, 40a
- ♿ gardens excellent, cemetery good
- 🍴 gardens on-site café

Famous Graves

Prospect Cemetery is the resting place of many of Ireland's most famous citizens: politicians Charles Stewart Parnell, Michael Collins, Eamon de Valera, Daniel O'Connell and Countess Markievicz, poet Gerard Manley Hopkins and writer Brendan Behan.

PHOENIX PARK (3, B2)

Dwarfing New York's Central Park and London's Hampstead Heath, Phoenix Park is one of the largest city parks in the world. Along with gardens, lakes and 300 deer, there are cricket and polo grounds, a motor-racing track and some fine 18th-century residences. A pleasant place to stroll during the day, it is unsafe after dark.

Near the Park Gate entrance is **People's Garden** (3, C3) dating from 1864, the **Victorian bandstand** in the Hollow and **Dublin Zoo** (p42). On the park's southern edge is a derelict, 18th-century **magazine fort** (3, B3).

Heading northwest along Chesterfield Ave, you'll find the **Áras an Uachtaráin** (3, B2), the Irish president's residence built in 1751, on the right. On the left, the **Papal Cross** (3, A2) marks the site where Pope John Paul II preached to more than a million people in 1979.

INFORMATION

- ☎ 677 0095
- 🖳 www.heritage ireland.ie
- € park grounds free, visitor centre €2.75/1.25-2/7
- ☯ visitor centre 10am-6pm Jun-Sep, 10am-5pm Oct, 9.30am-4.30pm Nov-Mar, 9.30am-5.30pm Apr-May
- ⓘ free 1hr tours of president's residence depart from visitor centre 10.30am-4pm Sat
- 🚌 visitor centre 37, 38, 39; park gate 10, 25, 26, 66, 67 68, 69
- ♿ good
- 🍴 visitor centre restaurant

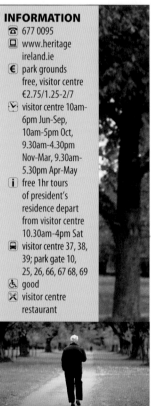

Murder in the Park

In 1882 Lord Cavendish, British chief secretary for Ireland, and his assistant were stabbed to death in Phoenix Park by members of a Fenian splinter nationalist group called The Invincibles. The assassins escaped but one of their comrades betrayed them and they were hanged at Kilmainham Gaol.

The polite way to murder the opposition is with your fine batting technique

Sights & Activities

MUSEUMS

Fry Model Railway (1, C1)
The railway engineer and draughtsman Cyril Fry began this collection of handmade models in the 1920s and '30s – now the 0-gauge replica of Ireland's transport system covers 240 sq metres. The model includes buses, trains, trams, barges, bridges and stations, and in the control room you can see how it all works.
☎ 846 3779 ⌨ www.visitdublin.com ✉ Malahide Castle Demesne, Malahide, Co Dublin € €6.25/3.75-5.25/17.50 ⏱ 10am-1pm & 2-5pm Mon-Thu & Sat, 2-6pm Sun & hols Apr-Oct 🚌 42 from city centre 🚉 Malahide 🚻 excellent

GAA Museum (4, F1)
Sporting enthusiasts will love this museum at Croke Park stadium, which explores the history of hurling, Gaelic football, camogie and handball from their ancient roots to the present day. Interactive screens let you test your own skills, listen to recordings from special matches and replay historic moments. You can also tour the grounds (12.30pm and 3pm Monday to Saturday, 1pm, 2.15pm and 3pm Sunday April to September; 2pm Monday to Saturday, 1pm and 3pm Sunday October to March).
☎ 855 8176 ⌨ http://museum.gaa.ie ✉ New Stand, Croke Park € €5/3.50/13, museum & stadium tour €8.50/6/21 ⏱ 9.30am-5pm Mon-Sat, from noon Sun (New Stand ticket holders only on match days) 🚌 3, 11, 11a, 16, 16a, 123 🚉 Connolly Station 🚻 excellent

Irish-Jewish Museum (3, E5)
Dublin's dwindling Jewish population is remembered through photographs, paintings, certificates, books and other memorabilia in this terrace house in the former Jewish district of Portobello. The museum recreates a typical 19th-century Dublin kosher kitchen, while upstairs is an old synagogue, in a state of disuse since the 1970s.
☎ 490 1857 ✉ 3-4 Walworth Rd € free ⏱ 11am-3.30pm Tue, Thu & Sun May-Sep; 10.30am-2.30pm Sun Oct-Apr 🚌 14, 15, 16, 19, 83, 122 🚻 limited

Museum of Banking (5, D2)
In the former Armoury and Guard House annexe to the Bank of Ireland, this small museum explores the history of banking, with particular emphasis on the bank's role in Ireland's economic and social development over the past 200 years.
☎ 671 1488 ⌨ www.bankofireland.ie ✉ Bank of Ireland Arts Centre, Foster Pl € €1.50/1 ⏱ by tour only 10am-3pm Tue-Fri 🚌 all city-centre buses

Bridge the Gap
A new architectural gem was unveiled in the city when the **James Joyce Bridge** (4, A5) opened, fittingly, on Bloomsday (16 June) 2003. Designed by renowned Spanish architect Dr Santiago Calatrava, the modernist marvel spans 40m over the Liffey and links Ellis Quay and Usher's Island, the site of Joyce's short story *The Dead*.

Discover the joys of hurling and camogie at the GAA Museum

**National Print Museum
(3, H4)** The print museum
pays homage to the skills,
tools and techniques of the
printer's art from the age
before computers. Ornate
printing presses, typesets,
Linotype machines and
historic newspaper pages
are on display, and you can
learn how books were once
bound and stitched.
☎ 660 3770 ✉ Garrison
Chapel, Beggars Bush
€ €3.50/2/7 ⏱ 10am-
5pm Mon-Fri, from noon
Sat & Sun May-Sep; from
10am Mon-Fri, from 2pm
Sat & Sun Oct-Apr 🚌 5,
7, 7a, 8, 45 🚆 Grand

Canal Dock, Landsdowne
Rd ♿ limited

**Old Jameson Distillery
(4, A5)** Housed in the original Jameson distillery where
the famous Irish whiskey
was produced from 1791
to 1966, the museum tells
the story of the site and the
drink. A heavy dose of marketing is thrown in, but fans
will enjoy the re-created
old factory, the detailed
explanations of the distilling
process and, of course, the
free glass of Jameson at the
end of the tour.
☎ 807 2355 ✉ Bow St,
Smithfield € €8/3.50-

6.25/19.50 ⏱ 9.30am-
5.30pm, by tour only
🚌 67, 67a, 68, 69, 79, 134
🚆 Smithfield ♿ good

**Waterways Visitor
Centre (3, H4)** Known to
Dubliners as 'the box in the
docks' for its cubist design,
Waterways Visitor Centre
provides an insight into
the history and importance
of Ireland's canal systems.
It uses video, models,
interactive computers and
displays to tell the story
of the waterways and the
people who worked on
them. The roof offers great
views of the area, which is
undergoing major renewal.
☎ 677 7510 🖥 www
.waterwaysireland.org
✉ Grand Canal Quay
€ €2.50/1.25-1.90/6.35
⏱ 9.30am-5.30pm Jun-
Sep, 12.30-5pm Wed-Sun
Oct-May, last admission
45min before closing
🚌 3 from O'Connell St
🚆 Grand Canal Dock
♿ limited

It's worth enduring the sales pitch for a glass of the good stuff at the Old Jameson Distillery

GALLERIES

Cross Gallery (4, B7)

Among the top-end antique stores of the Liberties, Cross is a relaxed modern gallery that promotes the work of both established and up-and-coming artists from Ireland and abroad. Expect abstract expressionism, muted landscapes and figurative work that tends towards the surreal.

☎ 473 8978 💻 www .crossgallery.ie ✉ 59 Francis St € free 🕑 10am-5.30pm Tue-Fri, 11am-4pm Sat 🚌 51b, 78a, 121, 123 ♿ good

Douglas Hyde Gallery (2, B2)

It might be on-campus at Trinity, but this ain't no half-baked student gallery. One of the city's more cutting-edge contemporary spaces, this gallery tends toward conceptual art, including installations and performance-driven pieces.

☎ 608 1116 💻 www .douglashydegallery.com ✉ Trinity College € free 🕑 11am-6pm Mon-Wed & Fri, to 7pm Thu, to 4.45pm Sat 🚌 all city-centre buses 🚉 Pearse Station, Tara St

Gallery of Photography (5, B3)

Ireland's premier photographic gallery, this place has ever-changing exhibits, often with Irish themes. Directly across the square you'll find the **National Photographic Archive** (☎ 603 0371; 🕑 10am-5pm Mon-Fri, to 2pm Sat), which displays mainly historical photographs from the National

Cross into the world of art

Library's collection.

☎ 671 4654 💻 www .irish-photography.com ✉ Meeting House Sq € free 🕑 11am-6pm Tue-Sat, from 1pm Sun 🚌 all city-centre buses ♿ good

Green on Red (2, E1)

This fashionable warehouse space houses cutting-edge, mainly Irish shows that range from prints, photography and sculpture to more esoteric installations.

☎ 671 3414 💻 www .greenonredgallery.com ✉ 26-28 Lombard St E € free 🕑 10am-6pm Mon-Fri, 11am-5pm Sat 🚌 1, 2, 3, 48a 🚉 Pearse Station

Kerlin Gallery (6, D3)

Hidden behind a nondescript door in a dingy little lane, the Kerlin Gallery is the ultimate statement in cool. Inside, the minimal-

ist space displays mainly conceptual and abstract art from some of Ireland's leading lights, including Dorothy Cross and Kathy Prendergast.

☎ 670 9093 💻 www .kerlin.ie ✉ Anne's La, Anne St S € free 🕑 10am-5.45pm Mon-Fri, 11am-4.30pm Sat 🚌 10, 14, 14a, 15

Kevin Kavanagh Gallery (5, B1)

On a backstreet behind the Morrison Hotel, Kevin Kavanagh's intimate gallery has a reputation of unearthing emerging Dublin artists. Kavanagh's eye has uncovered artists who now show at IMMA and abroad – catch them here first.

☎ 874 0064 💻 www .kevinkavanaghgallery.ie ✉ 66 Great Strand St € free 🕑 10am-5pm Tue-Sat, 11am-4pm Sat 🚌 37, 70, 134, 172 🚉 Jervis ♿ good

Lemonstreet Gallery (6, D2)

Lemonstreet specialises in contemporary printmaking, including limited-edition etchings, woodcuts, lithographs, screen prints and lino prints. Works by Francis Bacon, Michael Craig-Martin, Tony O'Malley and a host of local artists are available and you can order prints over the Internet.

☎ 671 0244 💻 www .lemonstreet.com ✉ Lemon St € free 🕑 10am-5.30pm Mon-Fri, 11am-5pm Sat 🚌 all city-centre buses

Origin Gallery (4, D8)

A relaxed space on the 1st floor of a Georgian terrace, Origin functions primarily as a showcase for artists who've stayed at the gallery's County Kerry retreat, Cill Rialaig. That means lots of landscape painting, but shows with various themes are also held.
☎ 478 5159
✉ 83 Harcourt St
€ free ⏲ 10.30am-5.30pm Mon-Fri, noon-4pm Sat 🚌 14, 15, 16, 19 🚇 Harcourt

Original Print Gallery

(5, C2) The gallery's back catalogue of work from 150 Irish and international printmakers is available for purchase, along with new, limited-edition work. You can also order prints online and have them shipped anywhere in the world.
☎ 677 3657 🖳 www .originalprint.ie ✉ 4 Temple Bar € free ⏲ 10.30am-5.30pm Mon- Fri, 11am-5pm Sat, 2-6pm Sun 🚌 all city-centre buses 🚇 Tara St

RHA Gallagher Gallery

(4, E8) Established in 1823, the Royal Hibernian Academy has four galleries, three dedicated to curated exhibits of Irish and international art, and a fourth, the Ashford Gallery, which promotes the work of Academy members and artists who haven't yet secured commercial representation. Works on show range from traditional to innovative.
☎ 661 2558 🖳 www .royalhibernianacademy .com ✉ 25 Ely Pl € free

⏲ 11am-5pm Tue-Sat, from 2pm Sun 🚌 10, 11, 13b, 51x ♿ excellent

Rubicon Gallery (6, D3)

In a beautiful bright Georgian space overlooking St Stephen's Green, the Rubicon is one of the city's more prestigious galleries, featuring mainly paintings by Irish gallery artists and up-and-comers but also sculpture and other media by international artists.
☎ 670 8055 🖳 www .rubicongallery.ie ✉ 1st fl, 10 St Stephen's Green € free ⏲ 11am-5.30pm Mon-Fri, to 4.30pm Sat 🚌 all city-centre buses

Solomon Gallery

In a restored Georgian salon on the top floor of the Powerscourt Centre (p54), Solomon Gallery has a reputation for showing fine figurative art including painting, ceramics, glass and mixed media. Along with contemporary pieces are traditional Irish period paintings. New exhibitions are launched frequently.
☎ 679 4237 🖳 www .solomongallery.com ✉ Powerscourt Centre, (6, C2) William St S € free ⏲ 10am-5.30pm Mon-Sat 🚌 all city-centre buses

Taylor Galleries (6, E3)

Founded in 1978, Taylor Galleries is the successor to both the Dawson and Waddington galleries. Housed in a fine Georgian building, contemporary artists shown include Louis le Brocquy, Tony O'Malley and John Doherty, while old-school works by Jack B Yeats and William Leech sometimes make an appearance.
☎ 676 6055
✉ 16 Kildare St € free ⏲ 10am-5.30pm Mon-Fri, 11am-3pm Sat 🚌 10, 11, 13 🚇 Pearse Station ♿ good

Temple Bar Gallery & Studios (5, C2)

Temple Bar Gallery & Studios has contemporary, thoughtful shows in a variety of media from a broad range of local and international artists. Set up in 1983 as an artist-run space, the gallery dedicates its upper floors to on-site studios and interesting solo or group shows from emerging painters, sculptors and mixed-media artists.
☎ 671 0073 🖳 www .templebargallery.com ✉ 5-9 Temple Bar ⏲ 11am-6pm Tue-Sat, to 7pm Thu 🚌 all city-centre buses 🚇 Tara St ♿ good

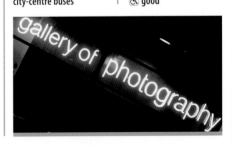

PLACES OF WORSHIP

Newman University Church (4, D8)
This Catholic church was built between 1854 and 1856 in an elaborate Byzantine style with multicoloured marble and copious gold leaf, making it very fashionable for society weddings. Cardinal Newman, who founded the city's first Catholic university next door at Newman House (p38), is honoured with a bust.
☎ 478 0616 ✉ 83 St Stephen's Green S € free ☾ 8am-6pm Mon-Sat 🚌 10, 11, 13, 14, 14a, 15a, 15b

St Audoen's Protestant Church (4, B6)
The only surviving medieval parish church in the city, St Audoen's was built between 1181 and 1212, though the site is thought to be much older. Enlarged in its 15th-century heyday, it shrunk to its present size in the 18th and 19th centuries, when the eastern wing and St Anne's Chapel were left to ruin. Today the chapel houses an excellent visitor centre, and sometimes runs guided tours.
☎ 677 0088 ✉ High St € €2/11.25/5.50 ☾ 9.30am-5.30pm Jun-Sep, last admission 4.45pm 🚌 51b, 78a, 123, 206 ♿ good

St Mary's Pro-Cathedral (4, D4)
Dublin's Catholic cathedral is tucked away on Marlborough St – a deliberately inconspicuous site. Built between 1816 and 1825, the cathedral's facade is modelled on the Temple of Theseus in Athens and its carved altar is also very impressive. Oddly, Marlborough St was once the biggest red-light district in Europe.
☎ 874 5441 🖥 www.procathedral.ie ✉ 83 Marlborough St € free ☾ 8am-7pm Mon-Sat, 8am-2pm Sun 🚌 27, 31b, 42a, 42b, 130 🚉 Connolly Station

St Michan's Church (4, A5)
Founded by Danes in 1095, major rebuilding in 1686 and 1828 left little of the original church here. The church has a fine oak organ that may have been played by Handel, but the star attraction is the underground vault, where buried bodies have been gruesomely mummified by the magnesium limestone walls.
☎ 872 4154 ✉ Church St Lower € €3.50/3 ☾ 10am-12.45pm & 2-4.45pm Mon-Fri, 10am-12.45pm Sat 🚌 134 ♿ limited

St Stephen's Church (3, G4)
Built in 1825 in Greek Revival style, St Stephen's is commonly known as the 'Peppercanister Church' because of its shape. It hosts classical concerts from time to time.
☎ 288 0663 ✉ Mount St Crescent € free ☾ services only, 11am Sun 🚌 5, 7, 7a, 8, 45, 46 🚉 Grand Canal Dock

St Werburgh's Church (6, A1)
On the west side of Dublin Castle, St Werburgh's Church stands on ancient foundations (probably 12th century). It was rebuilt in 1662, 1715 and again in 1759. Lord Edward Fitzgerald, a leader of the 1798 Rising, is interred in the vault.
☎ 478 3710 ✉ Werburgh St € free ☾ 10am-4pm Mon-Fri, ring bell for caretaker 🚌 50, 56a, 150

Whitefriar Street Carmelite Church (6, B3)
On the former site Carmelite monastery, this church houses a 16th-century Flemish oak statue of the Mother and Child, thought to be the only one of its kind to survive the Reformation. The altar contains the remains of St Valentine, donated by Pope Gregory XVI in 1835.
☎ 475 8821 ✉ 56 Aungier St € free ☾ 8am-6.30pm, to 8.30pm Tue, to 7.30pm Sun 🚌 16, 16a, 16c, 19, 19a, 65, 83 ♿ good

Dublin's Guilds
St Audoen's was one of several churches that served Dublin's crafts guilds from medieval times. Tradesfolk formed guilds to increase their influence and to establish standards for apprentices. Guilds often paid for the construction of chapels where Mass could be conducted at their request. The only remaining guildhall in Dublin, Tailor's Guild Hall, now houses the **National Trust** (4, B6; Back Lane).

NOTABLE BUILDINGS

Bank of Ireland (5, D2)
Built for the Irish Parliament, the Bank of Ireland moved in after the Act of Union in 1801. Though the House of Commons was remodelled, the House of Lords survived intact. Its Irish oak woodwork, mahogany standing clock, 18th-century crystal chandelier and tapestries are worth a look. Free tours are held on Tuesdays at 10.30am, 11.30am and 1.45pm.
☎ 671 1488, 677 6801 ⌨ www.bankofireland.ie ✉ College Green € free ⏱ 10am-4pm Mon-Fri, to 5pm Thu 🚍 all city-centre buses 🚈 Tara St ♿ limited

General Post Office
(4, D4) The GPO has played a starring role in Ireland's independence struggles. The 1916 Easter Rising leaders read their proclamation of a republic from its steps – the facade is still pockmarked from the subsequent clash and from fighting during the Civil War in 1922. Today the GPO still attracts protesting pressure groups and individuals on a personal crusade.
☎ 705 7000 ⌨ www.anpost.ie ✉ O'Connell St € free ⏱ 8am-8pm Mon-Sat 🚍 O'Connell St 🚈 Tara St ♿ limited

Government Buildings
(6, F3) The domed Government Buildings, built in an Edwardian interpretation of the Georgian style, were opened in 1911. Tours lasting around 40 minutes include the new wing, renovated in

the 1990s at a cost of £17.4 million, with the Taoiseach's office and the ceremonial staircase. The much more atmospheric old wing houses the cabinet room where Irish Free State ministers met for the first time.
☎ 662 4888 ⌨ www.taoiseach.gov.ie ✉ Merrion St Upper € free ⏱ 10.30am-3.30pm Sat, tickets from National Gallery on day of visit 🚍 7, 7a, 8, 45 🚈 Pearse Station ♿ by arrangement

National Library (6, F2)
Soak up the atmosphere of the library's gorgeous domed reading room (mentioned in Joyce's *Ulysses*). The extensive collection includes early manuscripts, 1st editions, maps and other items of interest. Temporary exhibitions are often held on the ground floor. On the 2nd floor is the Genealogical Office (p107).
☎ 603 0200 ⌨ www.nli.ie ✉ Kildare St € free ⏱ 10am-9pm Mon-Wed, to 5pm Thu-Fri, to 1pm Sat 🚍 10, 11, 13 ♿ limited

Sunlight Chambers
(5, A2) Sunlight Chambers, on the southern banks of the Liffey, stands out among the Georgian and modern architecture for its beautiful Art Nouveau friezework. Sunlight was a brand of soap was made by Lever Brothers, who built the late-19th-century building. The frieze shows the Lever Brothers' view of the world: men make clothes dirty, women wash them.
✉ Essex Quay 🚍 all city-centre buses

Windmill Lane Studios
(4, F5) Fans of Irish mega-band U2 still flock to the recording studio where the group produced their early albums. Much to the chagrin of other businesses in Windmill Lane, the entire street has become a graffiti homage to the band, despite signs pleading punters to 'spray it on the real wall'.
⌨ www.windmill.ie ✉ 4 Windmill La, Sir John Rogerson's Quay € free 🚍 1, 3 🚈 Pearse Station, Tara St

The sunlit Art Nouveau frieze of Sunlight Chambers

PARKS & GARDENS

**Airfield Trust Gardens
(1, C1)** Once the home of eccentric philanthropist sisters Letitia and Naomi Overend, the Airfield estate is now held in trust for public use. Though the house is closed to the public (except for the excellent café) the lovely 40-acre grounds with walled gardens, pet farm, vintage car museum and rose garden are great for a stroll.
☎ 298 4301 🖳 www .airfield.ie ✉ Kilmacud Rd Upper, Dundrum, Dublin 6 € €5/4/3 ⏰ 11am-5pm Tue-Sun Apr-Aug, 10am-4pm Tue-Sun Sep-Mar 🚌 44, 46a, 48a ♿ good

**Garden of Remembrance
(4, C3)** Established for the 50th anniversary of the 1916 Easter Rising, this peaceful garden commemorates those who sacrificed their lives in the long struggle for Irish independence. The centrepiece is a 1971 sculpture by Oisín Kelly depicting the myth of the Children of Lir, who were turned into swans by their wicked stepmother.
☎ 874 3074 🖳 www .heritageireland.ie ✉ Parnell Sq € free ⏰ 9.30am-dusk May-Sep, from 11am Oct-Apr 🚌 36, 40 🚉 Connolly Station ♿ limited

**Helen Dillon's Garden
(3, G6)** Gardening enthusiasts will enjoy a visit to award-winning gardener Helen Dillon's own dramatic garden at her 1830s home.

Inspired by Granada's Al-hambra, the walled garden is inventively landscaped with an impressive canal feature and colour-encoded exotic borders. Children are not allowed.
☎ 497 1308 ✉ 45 Sandford Rd, Ranelagh € €5 ⏰ 2-6pm Mar, Jul & Aug; 2-6pm Sun Apr, Jun, Sep & Oct 🚌 11, 13 🚉 Cowper

Herbert Park (3, H5)
This is a pleasant swathe of lush green lawns, ponds and flower beds near the Royal Dublin Society Showgrounds. Sandwiched between prosperous Ballsbridge and Donnybrook, the park runs alongside the River Dodder. There are tennis courts and a children's playground here too.
✉ Ballsbridge € free ⏰ dawn-dusk 🚌 5, 7, 7a, 8, 45, 46 🚉 Sandy-mount, Lansdowne Rd ♿ good

Iveagh Gardens (4, D8)
Once known to locals as the Secret Garden, the word is now out about the beautiful and ramshackle Iveagh Gardens, situated just behind Newman House; but you'll still find more space here than at nearby St Stephen's Green. Accessible from either Earlsfort Terrace or Harcourt St, the gardens were designed by Ninian Niven in 1863. Features of the beautifully landscaped gardens include a wonderfully rustic grotto, cascade, fountain, maze and rose garden.
☎ 475 7816 🖳 www .heritageireland.ie ✉ Clonmel St € free ⏰ 8am-dusk Mon-Sat, from 10am Sun 🚌 14, 14a, 15a, 15b 🚉 Harcourt ♿ good

Dublin's Canals

True Dubliners, it is said, are born within the confines of the two canals that encircle the inner city. The older Grand Canal, which began operation in 1779, stretches from Ringsend through south Dublin to the River Shannon in the centre of Ireland. Barges towed by horses carried cargo and passengers along the canal until 1960 when its commercial life came to an end. It is still used today by leisure craft. North Dublin's Royal Canal, built in 1790, never made money and was later sold to a railway company.

Both canals have pleasant stretches that are great for strolling or cycling. Join the **Royal Canal towpath** at North Strand Rd (3, G2), and follow it to the suburb of Clonsilla over 10km away. Or take the **Grand Canal towpath** west from Mount St Lower (3, G4) to the Robert Emmet Bridge (3, E5), stopping at one of the canalside pubs along the way.

LITERARY LANDMARKS

Dublin Writers Museum (4, C3) In a house once owned by the Jameson family (of whiskey fame), the museum celebrates Ireland's literary history. The displays could do with an update, both in presentation and content, but fans will enjoy the collection of letters, photographs, 1st editions and quirky memorabilia. ☎ 872 2077 🖳 www .writersmuseum.com ✉ 18 Parnell Sq N € €6.25/5.25/17.50 🕑 10am-6pm Mon-Fri, to 5pm Sat, 11am-5pm Sun Jun-Aug; 10am-5pm Mon-Sat, 11am-5pm Sun Sep-May 🚌 11, 13, 16, 19, 36, 40 🚉 Connolly Station

James Joyce Cultural Centre (4, D3) Joycean buffs will love this centre, in a fabulous Georgian house, which recreates the life and times of the great scribe through family portraits, letters and memorabilia as well as a reference library. Run by eccentric Joyce expert Senator David Norris, the house is the location of *Ulysses* dance instructor Denis Maginni's classes. The centre, not to be confused with the James Joyce Museum (p17), also runs Joyce tours. ☎ 878 8547 🖳 www .jamesjoyce.ie ✉ 35 Great George's St N € €3.80/2.50 🕑 9.30am-5pm Mon-Sat, from 12.30pm Sun 🚌 3, 10, 11, 13, 16, 19, 22, 123 🚉 Connolly Station

Oscar Wilde House (4, F7) The first Georgian residence built on Merrion Sq, No 1 was the home of surgeon Sir William Wilde, his wife (the poet Lady 'Speranza') and their son, Oscar, from 1855 to 1878. New owners, American College Dublin, now run tours of the restored 1st and 2nd floors, but information about the family is scant. ☎ 662 0281 🖳 www .amcd.ie ✉ 1 Merrion Sq N € €2.50 🕑 10.15 & 11.15am Mon, Wed & Thu 🚌 7, 8, 45, 84 🚉 Pearse Station

Shaw Birthplace (4, C9) The birthplace of playwright George Bernard Shaw is now an atmospheric museum, as interesting for its almost creepy recreation of Victorian middle-class life as for its literary links. The excellent self-guided audio tour is available in several languages. ☎ 475 0854 🖳 www .visitdublin.com ✉ 33 Synge St € €6.25/5.25/ 17.50 🕑 10am-1pm & 2-5pm Mon, Tue, Thu & Fri; 2-5pm Sat, Sun & hols May-Sep 🚌 16, 19, 122

Dublin Writers Museum, worth writing home about

Monumental Failures

Dublin's history is littered with public monuments that have been blown up, defaced, ridiculed and bungled. William III's statue on College Green was mutilated so often it was sold for scrap in 1929, as was one of George II soon after. In 1957 Lord Gough was blown off his horse in Phoenix Park, and in 1966 Lord Nelson's head exploded onto the footpath on O'Connell St. At the north end of Grafton St, the statue of **Molly Malone** (2, A2), with unlikely plunging neckline, represents the legendary cockles and mussels vendor who is the subject of Dublin's most famous song.

Dublin's latest civic project, the 120m-high spire sculpture, the **Monument of Light** (4, D4), replaced Nelson's Column on O'Connell St. Heated debate about its 'purpose' delayed its scheduled erection for millennium New Year's Eve by three years, though now most Dubliners appreciate its beauty, the scorn long forgotten.

GEORGIAN DUBLIN

City Hall (5, A3)

Restored to its Georgian glory, City Hall is adorned with neoclassical columns, a domed, gilded rotunda and patterned marble floors. Built by Thomas Cooley as the Royal Exchange from 1769 to 1779, the funerals of Michael Collins and Charles Stewart Parnell were held here. The *Story of the Capital* exhibition in the arched vaults traces Dublin's history through artefacts, models and multimedia displays.
☎ 672 2204 ▢ www .dublincity.ie/cityhall ✉ Cork Hill, Dame St € €4/2/10 ⏰ 10am- 5.15pm Mon-Sat, 2-5pm Sun 🚌 50, 50a, 54, 56a, 77, 77a, 123, 150 ♿ excellent

Custom House (4, E4)

A breathtaking Dublin landmark, Custom House was built to house the city's tax commissioners. James Gandon's first architectural triumph, the 18th-century building has a copper dome set with clock faces and neoclassical columns typical of the era. While the building now houses the Department of the Environment, the visitor centre explains Custom House's history.
☎ 888 2538 ✉ Custom House Quay € adult/ child/student/family €1.30/1.30/free/3.80 ⏰ 10am-12.30pm Mon- Fri, 2-5pm Sat & Sun mid- Mar–Oct; 10am-12.30pm Wed-Fri, 2-5pm Sun Nov–mid-Mar 🚆 Tara St, Connolly Station ♿ excellent, call ahead

Farmleigh (3, A1)

Another splendid string to architect James Gandon's bow, this fine Georgian- Victorian pile, once part of the Guinness estate, was restored to immaculate standard by the state in 2001. Only the ground floor, with a fantastic library and glass conserva- tory, is on view but the vast pleasure gardens with lake, walled and Japanese gardens are a delight to stroll.
☎ 815 5900 ▢ www .farmleigh.ie ✉ Phoenix Park, Castleknock € free ⏰ 10.30am-5.30pm Sat & Sun; call ahead, may be closed for official events 🚌 37 from city centre ♿ excellent, call ahead

Fitzwilliam Square

(4, E8) The smallest and last of Dublin's great Georgian squares, Fitzwilliam is home to a quiet and elegant block of immaculate terraces, boasting some elaborate doors and fanlights. While by day the square houses doctors' surgeries and solicitors' offices, by night prostitutes await custom. Only residents have access to the central garden.
✉ Dublin 2 🚌 10, 11, 13b, 46a, 58

Four Courts (4, B5)

With its 130m-long facade and neoclassical propor- tions, the Four Courts was built between 1786 and 1802 to the design of

Custom House, flying the flag for Ireland

James Gandon. In 1922 the building was captured by anti-Treaty republicans, and pro-Treaty forces shelled the site to try to dislodge them. Displays on the building's history and reconstruction are on the 1st floor. Court hearings can be observed from public galleries between 10am and 4pm only.

☎ 888 6441 ✉ Inns Quay € free ⏰ 9am-4.30pm Mon-Fri 🚌 134 🚆 Four Courts ♿ good

Leinster House (6, F3)

The Dáil and Seanad both meet at Leinster House, Ireland's parliament, when it sits for 90 days a year. Designed by Richard Cassels for the duke of Leinster, the Kildare St frontage is intended to look like a town house, while from Merrion St it appears to be a country estate.

☎ 618 3000, tour info 618 3271 🖥 www .oireachtas.ie ✉ Kildare St € free ⏰ public gallery open when parliament in session, usually Nov-May 🚌 7, 7a, 8, 10, 11, 13 🚆 Pearse Station ♿ good

Merrion Square (4, F7)

Merrion Sq is lined with stately Georgian buildings whose doors, peacock fanlights, ornate door knockers and foot-scrapers epitomise the elegance of the era. Former residents include the Wilde family (p36), WB Yeats and Daniel O'Connell. Its lush central gardens are perfect for a picnic or peaceful pit stop.

✉ Merrion Sq 🚌 5, 7, 7a, 8, 45 🚆 Pearse Station ♿ good

Mountjoy Square (4, D2)

Once the heart of Dublin's fashionable and affluent northside, today Mountjoy Sq is a reminder of the area's urban decay. Former residents include Sean O'Casey, who set his play *The Shadow of a Gunman* here, though he referred to it as Hilljoy Sq.

🚌 11, 16, 41 🚆 Connolly Station ♿ good

Newman House (4, D8)

Part of University College Dublin, Newman House consists of two exquisitely restored Georgian town houses with spectacular 18th-century stucco interiors. Don't miss

Merrion Sq resident

the Apollo Room and the Saloon by Paulo and Filipo LaFranchini, and later work by Robert West. Former students here include James Joyce and Eamon de Valera.

☎ 706 7422 ✉ 85-86 St Stephen's Green € €5/4 ⏰ by guided tour noon, 2pm, 3pm & 4pm Tue-Fri Jun-Sep 🚌 10, 11, 13, 14, 15a 🚆 St Stephen's Green

Number 29 (4, F7)

Built in 1794 for the widow of a wine merchant, Number 29 is a reconstruction of genteel Dublin home life c 1790 to 1820. From the rat traps in the basement kitchen to the handmade wallpaper upstairs, the attention to detail is impressive. Ironically, the museum only exists because the Electricity Supply Board, having demolished most of the block for its new offices, restored it in recompense.

☎ 702 6165 🖥 www .esb.ie ✉ 29 Fitzwilliam St Lower € €3.50/1.50, under 16 free ⏰ 10am-5pm Tue-Sat, from 2pm Sun 🚌 6, 7, 8, 10, 45 🚆 Pearse Station

By George

The Georgian period is roughly defined as the years between the accession of George I in 1714 and the death of George IV in 1830. Its inspiration was the work of the 16th-century Italian architect Andrea Palladio, who believed reason and the principles of classical antiquity should govern building.

In Dublin, the austere formality of the style was tempered by the use of coloured doors, delicate fanlights, intricate ironwork and exuberant interior plasterwork.

SEASIDE SUBURBS

Bray (1, C2)

The Brighton of Dublin, Bray has a long seafront parade of fast-food places, tacky amusement arcades, candyfloss vendors and happily screeching kids. Developed in the 1850s when the railway arrived, Bray is 19km south of Dublin. Home to a **Martello tower** owned by Bono, Bray also has fine views of the Wicklow Mountains and an 8km **cliff walk** around Bray Head to Greystones further south. The centre of indoor movie production in Ireland is **Ardmore Studios** on Herbert Rd, host to practically every high-profile movie from *The Commitments* to *My Left Foot*. Catch the DART to Bray.

Clontarf (1, C1)

Just 5km northeast of the centre, Clontarf is a pretty bayside suburb whose main attractions are birds and golf. The **North Bull Wall**, which extends about 1km into Dublin Bay, was built in 1820 to stop Dublin Harbour from silting up. Marshes and dunes developed behind the wall, creating **North Bull Island** which is now a Unesco biosphere reserve. The bird population can reach 40,000 – watch for shelducks, curlews and oystercatchers on the mud flats – and a range of plants and other animals can be seen. An **interpretive centre** (☎ 833 8341; admission free; ☼ times vary, call ahead) on the island is reached by walking across the 1.5km-long northern causeway. Transport to the island is poor. Catch the DART to Raheny, from where it's a 40-minute walk to the northern causeway, or catch bus No 130 from Abbey St Lower to the Bull Wall stop, within a 25-minute walk.

Dalkey (1, C2)

In medieval times Dalkey was Dublin's most important port town and boasted seven castles, of which only two remain. Today the quaint village is home to Dublin's rich and famous, including several members of U2, racing driver Damon Hill and film director Neil Jordan. As well as good restaurants and pubs on Castle St, the village main drag, the coastline and beaches nearby are superb.

The roofless **Archibold's Castle** on Castle St is closed except at Christmas, when a nativity crib is open to visitors. Across the road is the 15th-century **Dalkey Castle Heritage Centre**, which houses an interesting **visitor centre** (☎ 285 8366; €6/5/16; ☼ 9.30am-5pm Mon-Fri, from 11am Sat, Sun & hols). Exhibits explain the castle's defence systems, the history of the area's transport and various myths and legends. The remains of the 11th-century **St Begnet's church & graveyard** are also here.

The waters around **Dalkey Island** are popular with scuba divers – catch one of the small boats touting for business at Coliemore Harbour. To get to Dalkey from Dublin, catch the DART.

Howth (1, C1)

Howth (rhymes with 'both'), at the northern end of Dublin Bay, offers visitors a quaint fishing village, walks on the windswept peninsula and a nearby island to explore. **Howth town**, 15km northeast of central Dublin and accessible by DART, has a pleasant port with three piers, some good pubs and excellent fish and chip joints.

Looming above it is the **Hill of Howth**, wonderful for a leisurely half- or full-day's walk with views of Dublin city and the bay. In spring the peninsula is ablaze with unusual wildflowers, and seabirds caterwaul around

Stunning view from Howth to Ireland's Eye (foreground) and Lambay Island (background)

the shore. Grab the Howth Heritage Trust's *The Howth Peninsula* map and guide from Eason's (p64) in O'Connell St before you go.

About 1.5km offshore is **Ireland's Eye**, a rocky seabird sanctuary with the ruins of a 6th-century monastery. There's a Martello tower at the island's northwestern end, while at the eastern end a spectacular rock face plummets into the sea. Seals can also be spotted. **Doyle & Sons** (☎ 831 4200) runs boats out to the island from the East Pier of Howth Harbour during summer from around 10.30am on weekends. Return trips cost €8.

Malahide   (1, C1)

A pretty town with a marina and several good restaurants, Malahide's main attraction is **Malahide Castle** (☎ 846 2184; €6/3.50-5/16.50), set in 1 sq km of parklands. The castle served as the Talbot family home from 1185 to 1976 and incorporates a hotchpotch of architectural styles from the 12th to the 18th centuries. On the grounds is the **Fry Model Railway** (p29) and **Tara's Palace** (☎ 846 3779; admission by donation; ◷ 10.45am-4.45pm Mon-Sat, 11.30am-5.30pm Sun Apr-Sep), an elaborate, over-sized doll's house whose rooms are furnished with fittings from around the world. The **Talbot Botanic Gardens** (☎ 872 7777; €4; ◷ 2-5pm May-Sep), also within the grounds, has a varied collection of plants, many from the southern hemisphere. Catch bus No 42 from Busáras or the DART from Connolly Station.

Malahide Castle, a regular family home...

QUIRKY DUBLIN

Casino at Marino (3, H1)
Roman temple from the outside and kooky Georgian house inside, the Casino at Marino is one of Ireland's finest – and weirdest – Palladian buildings. The house was built by Sir William Chambers for the eccentric James Caulfield (1728–99), later earl of Charlemont. While externally the building appears to contain just one room, the interior is a convoluted maze of rooms.
☎ 833 1618 ⌨ www .heritageireland.ie
✉ Malahide Rd, Marino
€ €2.75/1.25-1.90/6.35
🕑 10am-6pm Jun-Sep; to 5pm May & Oct; noon-4pm Sat & Sun Nov & Dec, Feb-Apr (to 5pm Apr); last tour 45min before closing
🚌 20a, 20b, 27, 27b, 42, 42c, 123 🚉 Clontarf Rd

Chimney (4, A4)
Re-create Willy Wonka's final scene by shuttling up a 185ft glass lift to Dublin's first and only 360-degree observation tower. OK, so you don't burst into Pinewood Studios, but on a clear day you can view the entire city, the sea and the mountains to the south from the comfort of this converted 1895 Jameson distillery chimney.
☎ 817 3838
✉ Smithfield Village
€ adult/student €5/3.50
🕑 10am-5pm Mon-Sat, 11am-5.30pm Sun
🚌 67, 67a, 68, 69, 79, 134 🚉 Smithfield

Melt (5, B3)
Dublin's first walk-in health and beauty shop offers you the chance to luxuriate in a 10-minute cranio-sacral or aromatherapy massage, take an Aveda facial, or a kinesiology session or stock up on Chinese medicines at the herb bar. Ring ahead for consultations.
☎ 679 8786 ✉ 2 Temple Lane S 🕑 9am-9pm Mon-Fri, 10am-6pm Sat, noon-6pm Sun
🚌 all cross-city

A Sporting Chance
The Golden Pages is a useful place to find listings of sports facilities near you. Dublin Tourism publishes the free *Golfing Around Dublin* guide, available at their office in Suffolk St. Check out www.golfdublin.com for information about the city's public courses. The following associations can also point you in the right direction:
Basketball Ireland (☎ 459 0211; www.basketballireland.ie)
Irish Sailing Association (☎ 280 0239; www.sailing.ie)
Irish Squash (☎ 625 1145; www.irishsquash.com)
Irish Waterski Federation (☎ 285 5205; www.iwsf.ie)
Pitch & Putt Union of Ireland (☎ 625 1110; www.iol.ie/ppui)
Tennis Ireland (☎ 884 4010; www.tennisireland.ie)

Flex those muscles at the following sporting venues around town:
Ashtown Riding Stables (3, A1; ☎ 838 3807) Trail ride in Phoenix Park.
Deer Park Golf Course (☎ 832 2624) Tee off in the grounds of Howth Castle in Howth town (1, C1).
Herbert Park Tennis Club (3, H5) Love all in leafy suburb, Herbert Park.
Irish National Sailing School (☎ 284 4195; www.inss.ie) Tack off in Dun Laoghaire (1, C1).
Markievicz Leisure Centre (4, E5; ☎ 672 9121) Swim and gym on Townsend St.
Surfdock (3, H4; ☎ 668 3945; www.surfdock.ie) Board the breeze at Grand Canal Dock.

DUBLIN FOR CHILDREN

Dublin is a reasonably child-friendly city but it does have its drawbacks. The main problem is infrastructure – poor transport means lots of walking, there are few public spots to stop and rest (particularly on the northside), and trendification means many pubs are not as family-friendly as they used to be. There's also a dearth of public toilets in the city centre, although the major shopping centres have toilets and baby change facilities. On the upside, the increased wealth of Dubliners has spurred a variety of children's activities. And a good number of restaurants accept child diners, though it's best to arrive early in the evening.

Ark (5, B3) A four-storey cultural centre with a theatre, gallery and workshop, the Ark is aimed at kids aged four to 14. Its programmes promote an interest in science, the environment and the arts, and its core staff are supplemented by artists from a variety of disciplines. There are plenty of exhibitions, workshops and artistic pro-

Get down at the Ark

ductions on offer, but book well ahead to ensure a place. ☎ 670 7788 🖳 www .ark.ie ✉ 11a Eustace St € €4.50-8.50 ⏲ Sat & Sun, activity times vary 🚌 all cross-city buses ♿ excellent

Dublin Zoo (3, C2) The second-oldest public zoo in Europe, Dublin Zoo is home to more than 700 animals, including rhinos, gorillas, leopards, penguins and polar bears. Apart from the animal antics, kids will enjoy the regular feedings, the mini-train ride through the grounds, the new African safari plains and, if all else fails, the big playground. ☎ 677 1425 🖳 www .dublinzoo.ie ✉ Phoenix Park € €11/7/32 ⏲ 9.30am-6pm Mon-Sat, 10.30am-6pm Sun May-Sep; 9.30am-4pm Mon-Fri, 9.30am-5pm Sat, 10.30am-5pm Sun Oct-Apr

🚌 10 from O'Connell St (4, D4), 25 or 26 from Abbey St Middle ♿ good

Dvblinia (4, B6) Inside what was once Christ Church's Synod Hall, Dvblinia recreates medieval Dublin using models, music, streetscapes and interactive displays. Adults might find it a bit kitsch, but kids will love the hands-on archae-ology room and re-created medieval fair – with simple but fun activities at each stall. Make your own brass rubbing, try on armour or try to knock medieval man's nose with a ball. You can climb St Michael's Tower for panoramic views of the city. ☎ 679 4611 ✉ Christ Church € €5.75/4.75/17, under 5 free ⏲ 10am-5pm Apr-Sep; 11am-4pm Mon-Sat, 10am-4.30pm Sun Oct-Mar 🚌 51b, 78a, 123, 206 ♿ good

Lambert Puppet Theatre The puppets are all hand-made, the theatre has been running since 1972, and the performers span three generations of the same family. It's not hard to see why Lambert is a Dublin institution. Shows include old favourites like *Hansel and Gretel* and newer works

Other Kids Stuff

Some other choice activities to keep the children happy can be found at:

- Weekend or holiday programmes at the National Gallery of Ireland (p12)
- National Museum (p11, p21, p26)
- Irish Museum of Modern Art (p19)
- Temple Bar Diversions festival (p16)

written by the company. During the International Puppet Festival in September international acts take the stage with their weird and wonderful creations. ☎ 280 0974 🖥 www .lambertpuppettheatre .com ✉ Clifton La, Monkstown (1, C1), Co Dublin € €9.50/8.50 🕑 box office 10am-5pm, puppet show 3.30pm Sat & Sun 🚉 Monkstown ♿ excellent

Marlay House & Park
(1, C2) Marlay Park, 9km south of the city centre, is a wonderful 83-hectare open space, with 17th-century buildings, wooded area, abundant wildlife, walled garden, sculpture trail and craft centre. Kids will especially love the fairy bridge, massive playground, skateboard park and, in summer, the mini train (3pm to 5pm May to September) that jostles around a field track. ✉ Grange Rd, Rathfarn-ham, Dublin 14 € free 🕑 10am-dusk 🚌 15c, 16, 16a, 48 ♿ good

National Aquatic Centre
(1, B1) Opened in March 2003 to accommodate the Special Olympics World Summer Games is the largest indoor water park in Europe. Besides its Olympic-size competition pool it has fantastic water roller coasters, wave and surf machines, a leisure pool and all types of flumes. Be prepared to join the shivering line of children queuing for slides on weekend afternoons. ☎ 646 4300 🖥 www .nac.ie ✉ Snugborough

Rd, Blanchardstown, Dublin 15 € €9/7/25.60 🕑 11am-10pm Mon-Fri, 9am-8pm Sat & Sun 🚌 38a from Hawkins St (5, F1)

National Sealife Centre
The once tired-looking National Aquarium was taken over by a British company and is now a much more pleasant place to visit. Aquariums are stocked with 70 different sea and freshwater species, from sea horses to sharks. ☎ 286 6939 ✉ Strand Rd, Bray (1, C2) € €8.50/5.50/27, under 3 free 🕑 10am-6pm, to 6.30pm Sat & Sun Apr-Oct; 11am-5pm Mon-Fri, 10am-6pm Sat & Sun Nov-Mar 🚉 Bray ♿ good

National Wax Museum
(4, C3) Dublin's version of the ubiquitous wax museum combines the usual parade of stars with Irish historical figures. Jack and the Bean-stalk, Aladdin, the Flintstones and ET will suit the youngest, while older kids who aren't squeamish might prefer the Chamber of Horrors. Joyce, Yeats, Robert Emmet and

several Irish presidents are on show, but kids will probably prefer Michael Jackson, Madonna and U2. ☎ 872 6340 ✉ Granby Row, Parnell Sq € €7/5-6 🕑 10am-5.30pm Mon-Sat, from noon Sun 🚌 all cross-city buses 🚉 Connolly Station ♿ limited

Newbridge House & Farm (1, C1) Newbridge House combines a historic Georgian manor with a large traditional farm. The house has an elaborate interior, with fine plasterwork, period furniture, a museum and an ornate coach in the stables. The self-sufficient, 18th-century farm has cows, pigs and birds, as well as rare breeds like the Conne-mara pony, Jacob sheep and some exotic chickens with punk hairdos. ☎ 843 6534 ✉ Donabate, Co Dublin € house €6.50/3-5.50/17.50, farm €3.50/2/8 🕑 10am-5pm Tue-Sat, 2-6pm Sun Apr-Sep; 2-5pm Sat & Sun Oct-Mar 🚌 33b from Eden Quay (4, E4) 🚉 Donabate ♿ limited

Out & About

WALKING TOURS
Perambulate with Pints

Begin at the hip but low-key **Dice Bar** (**1**; p83) on Queen St, turn onto Arran Quay and head right over the bridge to the **Brazen Head** (**2**; p85) on Bridge St, turn right onto the quays and down to Wellington Quay

'Hmm, another beer here, or at Grogan's?'

and the **Octagon Bar** (**3**; p84) in the Clarence. Leave by the Essex St entrance, turn left and then right to walk south to Dame St and Great George's St S. Take the first laneway left off Great George's St S down to the magnificent **Stag's Head** (**4**; p87). Retrace your steps back onto Great George's St S, and head to the **Globe** (**5**; p83). Take a left around the corner of George's St Arcade and into the loud and

lively **Market Bar** (**6**; p84). Turning left onto Drury St, hang a right at Castle Market and into bohemian **Grogan's** (**7**; p85). Then cross over Clarendon and Grafton Sts, nipping into **Davy Byrne's** (**8**; ☎ 677 5217; 21 Duke St) for a top-up of oysters and Guinness before hitting the snug at **Kehoe's** (**9**; p87). Turn right at Dawson St into cosmopolitan **Ron Blacks** (**10**; p84) and further up into Dublin's smallest pub **Dawson Lounge** (**11**; ☎ 677 5217; 25 Dawson St), before turning left at St Stephen's Green N, continuing down Merrion Row to take in some tunes at **O'Donoghue's** (**12**; p88).

A couple of pints of the good stuff and you'll be seeing double too

distance 2.5km **duration** 2hr
▶ **start** 🚌 25, 25a, 51, 66, 70, 79, 90, 172
● **end** 🚌 10, 25x, 49x, 51x

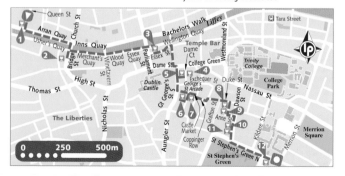

The Liberties to Kilmainham

Start outside **Dublin Corporation** (**1**) on Wood Quay, and take Fishamble St south to **Christ Church Cathedral** (**2**; p15). Backtrack to Werburgh St and **St Werburgh's Church** (**3**; p33). Continue south, turn right at Kevin St Upper, then right again at St Patrick's Close for **Marsh's Library** (**4**; p25) and **St Patrick's Cathedral** (**5**; p23). Cross Patrick St and head to the antique shops of Francis St. Turn right at Thomas Davis St to Back Lane and the **Tailor's Guild Hall** (**6**; p33). Turn left at Cornmarket, passing **St Audoen's Catholic Church** (**7**) and **St Audoen's Protestant Church** (**8**; p33), both on your right. Continue west along Cornmarket, passing **John's Lane Augustinian Church** (**9**) and **St**

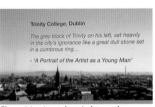

Trinity College, Dublin

The grey block of Trinity on his left, set heavily in the city's ignorance like a great dull stone set in a cumbrous ring…

- 'A Portrait of the Artist as a Young Man'

The writing is on the window at the Guinness Storehouse

Catherine's (**10**) outside which the patriot Robert Emmet was beheaded. Turn left at Crane St and follow the signs to the **Guinness Storehouse**

(**11**; p13) where you can pause for a snack and pint. Turn right at Grand Canal Pl, then right again at Echlin St to rejoin Thomas St opposite the **St James's Gate Brewery** (**12**; p13). Cross the road, veer right onto Bow Lane W and turn right again into Steeven's Lane. **St Patrick's Hospital** (**13**) and **Dr Steeven's Hospital** (**14**) are both on your left. Turn left at St John's Rd W. At Heuston Station turn left into Military Rd for the **Irish Museum of Modern Art** (**15**; p19).

You'll need a rest when you get to IMMA

---

distance 4.4km **duration** 2hr

▶ **start** 🚌 50, 66, 77, 121, 123

● **end** 🚌 68, 69, 78a, 79, 90, 123

Waterside Wander

Start at the **Bleeding Horse** (**1**; p117) on Camden St Lower, built in 1710 as a farrier inn, and walk south to the **Portobello** (**2**; ☎ 465 2715;

Box in the Docks; Waterways Visitor Centre

33 Richmond St S), a pub built to house canal workers. Turning left at the Grand Canal, begin your stroll along the towpath, passing several old locks that still operate. About 300m past Leeson St Lower, there's a statue of poet **Patrick Kavanagh** (**3**) relaxing on a bench. At Macartney Bridge, turn right onto Baggot St and refuel at **Searsons** (**4**; ☎ 660 0330; 42 Upper Baggot St). Continue east on the canal, diverting left at Mount Street Cres for **St Stephen's Church** (**5**; p33). Back on the towpath, turn right at Northumberland Rd, then left at Haddington Rd for the **National Print Museum** (**6**; p30). Turn left at Grand Canal St Upper and divert right to Barrow St, where you can climb the steps of the DART station to see an ornate Victorian gas ring. Retrace your steps, turning right at Grand Canal Quay for **Waterways Visitor Centre** (**7**; p30). Turn left at Pearse St, right at Cardiffs Lane and left again at Sir John Rogerson's Quay. Turn left at Windmill Lane to see **Windmill Lane Studios** (**8**; p34), where U2 produced their early albums, then rest on a bench at City Quay with views of Custom House (p37).

Stop to chat with poet Patrick Kavanagh

distance 5.5km **duration** 3hr

▶ **start** 🚌 16, 16a, 19, 19a, 65, 83

● **end** 🚌 Tara Street

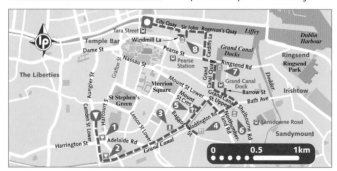

Take a Walk on the Northside

From **Mountjoy Sq** (**1**; p38), head southwest down Gardiner Pl turning left into Great George's St N, one of the best-preserved Georgian streets in the north. Visit the **Cobalt Cafe & Gallery** (**2**; p68) and **James Joyce Cultural Centre** (**3**; p36). Turn right onto Parnell St, pass the **Charles Stewart Parnell statue** (**4**) and do a clockwise loop of Parnell Sq. You'll pass the **Rotunda Hospital** (**5**) on the south side, and the **Hugh Lane Gallery** (**6**; p24) and **Dublin Writers Museum** (**7**; p36) on the north side. Near the towering **Abbey Presbyterian Church** (**8**) is the **Garden of Remembrance** (**9**; p35). Continue around the square past the **Gate Theatre** (**10**; p91) to O'Connell St where you'll find the **James Joyce statue** (**11**) and the **General Post Office** (**12**; p34). Continue down O'Connell St to the **Daniel O'Connell monument** (**13**) and right onto the quays, stopping to admire **Ha'penny Bridge** (**14**). Refuel at the **Winding Stair** (**15**; p65, p69) café and bookshop, then continue along the quays, admiring the view, to James Gandon's dramatic **Four Courts** (**16**; p37). At Church St turn right to see the grisly vaults at **St Michan's Church** (**17**; p33).

The dramatic Four Courts building

distance 3km **duration** 2hr

▶ **start** 🚌 11, 16, 41 🚉 Connolly Station

● **end** 🚌 134

Ha'Penny Bridge over the Liffey

DAY TRIPS
Glendalough (1, C3)

Spectacularly set in a deep valley beside two ancient lakes, Glendalough (*glen*-da-loh) is an ancient monastic settlement that somehow retains its magic, despite the hordes of tourists who visit. The Visitor Centre sets the scene with some interesting displays, a video on ancient Irish monasteries and a model of Glendalough in its prime.

One of the country's most important sites, Glendalough was founded by St Kevin in the 6th century AD. From this time on it was renowned for the monastic settlement, where hermit monks retired to contemplate in the quiet solitude of the valley. The settlement survived Viking raids and an English incursion in 1398, before it was finally dissolved during the Reformation.

The ruins here include a **10th-century round tower**, the **Cathedral of St Peter and St Paul**, a fine **high cross** and **St Kevin's Church**, a stone masterpiece.

INFORMATION
54km south of Dublin

- 🚌 St Kevin's Bus Service (☎ 281 8119), 11.30am from Royal College of Surgeons (4, D7)
- ☎ 0404-45325
- 💻 www.glendalough.connect.ie
- € Visitor Centre €2.75/1.25-2/7
- 🕐 Visitor Centre 9.30am-4.30pm, to 5.15pm mid-Mar–mid-Oct
- ℹ️ *Walking Trails of Glendalough* (50c), *Visitor's Guide* (80c)
- 🍴 Wicklow Heather Restaurant (☎ 0404-45157), Laragh

The aptly named Round Tower

St Kevin's Church, also called St Kevin's Kitchen. Was St Kevin the first Irish celebrity chef?

Green Rd takes you to the ruins and breathtaking scenery of **Upper Lake** to the west. The remains of an early Christian **stone fort**, the 11th-century **Reefert Church** and **St Kevin's Bed**, a 2m-deep cave where the saint is said to have slept, are scattered around the lake's southeastern edge.

Those with monastic tendencies might like the **Heritage Retreat Centre** (☎ 0404-45140; per night €40), which rents out individual hermitages to those seeking solitude and quiet contemplation. The one-person, self-catering accommodation includes a bed, bathroom, small kitchen and open fire but no electricity.

Irish National Stud & Japanese Gardens (1, A2)

In the heartland of Ireland's hugely successful horse-breeding and racing industry, the National Stud was founded in 1900 by Colonel William Hall-Walker (of the Johnnie Walker distilling family). Home to some of Ireland's top breeding stallions, as well as a museum, you don't need to be a racing aficionado to appreciate a visit - the setting is beautiful.

The Japanese Gardens next door were laid out by master gardener Tasso Eida and his son Minoru in 1906. The gardens chart the journey of life through a series of symbolic landmarks and are considered to be among the finest Japanese gardens in Europe.

INFORMATION
60km southwest of Dublin
- 🚌 Bus Éireann (p112; ☎ 836 6111) to Kildare, several departures daily
- 🚆 Arrow line from Heuston to Kildare
- ☎ Irish National Stud 045-521251, Japanese Gardens 045-521617
- 🖥 www.irish-national-stud.ie
- ✉ Tully, Co Kildare
- € €8.50/4.50-6.50/18, incl gardens
- 🕙 9.30am-5pm mid-Feb–mid-Nov
- ⓘ guided tours of stud hourly
- ✗ Silken Thomas (☎ 045-522252), Market Sq, Tully

Russborough House (1, B2)

One of Ireland's finest stately homes, Russborough House was designed by Richard Cassels and built between 1740 and 1751. The magnificent Palladian villa's granite central building is flanked by two wings, connected by curving, pillared colonnades. Inside, the style is exuberantly baroque, with ornate plasterwork by the LaFranchini brothers and period fittings and furnishings.

The house was taken by Irish forces during the 1798 Rising and then by government forces, who only left in 1801 after a furious Lord Russborough challenged the commander of the British forces, Lord Tyrawley, to a duel 'with blunderbusses and slugs in a sawpit'. In 1952 the house was bought by Sir Alfred Beit of De Beers, who brought his remarkable art collection with him. Works by Goya, Gainsborough, Rubens and Vermeer still hang in the grand rooms, though security is tight after high-profile robberies in 1974 and 1986. Many of the more valuable works now hang in the National Gallery (p12).

INFORMATION
40km southwest of Dublin
- 🚌 65 from Eden Quay (4, E4; 6am-11.15pm, 10 daily)
- ☎ 045-865239
- ✉ 5km southwest of Blessington, Co Wicklow
- € €6/2.50-4
- 🕙 10am-5pm May-Sep, 10am-5pm Sun & hols Apr & Oct
- ✗ on-site tearoom

Powerscourt (1, C2)

About 1km from the picturesque village of Enniskerry is Powerscourt House, designed by Richard Cassels on the site of a 13th-century castle. Much of the house accidentally burnt down in 1974 and has not been restored to its former glory. The ballroom is the only original room remaining. The house contains a small **historical exhibition**, several **craft shops** and an excellent **restaurant**, but the real attraction is the estate's fabulous 20-hectare garden.

The terraced gardens descending the hill in front of the house are backed by the peak of the 506m-high Sugarloaf Mountain. The **Italianate front gardens** were begun in the 19th century when an enormous number of trees were planted. The grounds were adorned with elaborate statues and ironwork collected by the Wingfield family who held court here for more than 350 years.

The **Japanese Garden** includes maples, azaleas and palms, as well as a pagoda, wooden bridges and stone lanterns. One of the oldest parts of the estate is the **Walled Gardens**, with Venetian gates and multicoloured rose bushes. One of the strangest features is the **Pet Cemetery**, complete with headstones mourning the passing of Tiny the dachshund and Eugenie the Jersey cow.

A 5km walk or shuttle-bus ride away is the 130m high **Powerscourt Waterfall** (€4/3-3.50; 🕙 9.30am-7pm Mar-Oct, 10am-dusk Nov-Feb), the highest in Britain and Ireland. It's most impressive after heavy rain.

INFORMATION

22km south of Dublin

- 🚌 44 from Hawkins St (5, F1) to Enniskerry
- 🚆 DART to Bray, then bus No 85 to Enniskerry. Alpine shuttle bus (☎ 286 2547) from Enniskerry or Bray station to house & waterfall.
- ☎ 204 6000
- 🖥 www.powerscourt.ie
- ✉ Enniskerry, Co Wicklow
- € house €2.50/1.60-2.20, garden €6/3.50-5.50, house & garden €8/4-7
- 🕙 house & garden 9.30am-5.30pm
- 🍽 Avoca Restaurant on-site; Poppies Country Cooking (☎ 282 8869), The Square, Enniskerry

Powerscourt's glory was diminished in a fire 30 years ago; imagine what it was like before!

ORGANISED TOURS

Dublin has loads of tours to choose from, with themes from literary landmarks to ghostly tales. Day trips outside Dublin are easy, with a variety of coach and rail tours that travel as far away as the Aran Islands in Galway.

Bus

Dublin Bus (4, D4)

A hop-on, hop-off tour around the major sights of Dublin. The whole tour lasts around 1¼ hours and you can get on and off at any of the 16 designated stops.
☎ 872 0000, 873 4222 🖳 www.dublinbus.ie ✉ 59 O'Connell St Upper € €12.50/6 ⏱ 9.30am-5pm

Bus Éireann

Day trips go to major nearby attractions, including Glendalough (p48), Powerscourt (p50), Newgrange, the Boyne Valley and Avoca – setting for TV hit *Ballykissangel*. Book at Dublin Tourism (5, D3), Busáras (4, E4) or online. Tours leave from Dublin Bus (4, D4).
☎ 836 6111 🖳 www.buseireann.ie ✉ 59 O'Connell St Upper € most tours €30/19.50

Mary Gibbons Tours

(6, A6) Full-day tours of Powerscourt (p50) and Glendalough (p48), as well as a celebrated tour of the Boyne Valley, including Newgrange and the Hill of Tara, the ancient seat of the Irish high kings. All tours depart from outside Dublin Tourism (5, D3).
☎ 283 9973 ✉ Suffolk St € €28 ⏱ Powerscourt & Glendalough 10.45am Thu, Sat & Sun; Boyne Valley 10.45am Mon-Wed & Fri

Wild Coach Tours

Small Mercedes coaches take you to Wicklow/Glendalough (p48), Malahide Castle or Powerscourt (p50), with lots of diversions along interesting scenic routes that the bigger buses usually miss. Excellent, energetic guides create a fun and friendly atmosphere. Tours have a variety of pick-up points.
☎ 475 3313 🖳 www.discoverdublin.ie € Wicklow €28/ 25, Powerscourt or Malahide €20/16 ⏱ Wicklow 9am, Powerscourt 1.30pm, Malahide 9am

Horse & Carriage

Horse & Carriage Tours

Along the west side of St Stephen's Green (6, D3) you can pick up a horse and carriage with a driver/commentator for a tour around town. Most last half an hour but you can negotiate with the driver for longer trips. Carriages hold four or five people.
✉ St Stephen's Green, near Fusiliers' Arch € around €40 per 30min

Kooky

Viking Splash Tours

(4, B7) Possibly Dublin's kookiest tour, Viking Splash takes you out on a reconditioned WWII amphibious vehicle that goes to Viking sites around the city before splashing into the Grand Canal Basin for a water tour. All the while your 'craaazy' guide in Viking costume spins tales of the city.
☎ 707 6000 🖳 www.vikingsplashtours.com ✉ Bull Alley St € €14.50-15.95/7.95-8.95 ⏱ Feb-Nov up to 17 tours daily

Literary, Music & History

Dublin Footsteps Walking Tours (6, D2)

A gentle two-hour walk through Dublin's Georgian and literary past, bringing you to Merrion Sq (p38) and St Stephen's Green (p18). Anecdotes about Joyce, Wilde, Shaw and Yeats highlight various points of interest. The tour ends back at Bewley's, with a free cuppa.
☎ 496 0641, 269 7021 ✉ James Joyce Room, Bewley's Café, 78 Grafton St € €9 ⏱ 10.30am Mon, Wed, Fri & Sat Jun-Sep

James Joyce Cultural Centre (4, D3)

The centre conducts one-hour walking tours of North Dublin, exploring Joyce's writings, his inspirations and various *Ulysses* landmarks. Tours depart from, and include, the James Joyce Cultural Centre (p36). Book in advance.
☎ 878 8547 🖳 www.jamesjoyce.ie ✉ 35 Great George's St N € €10/9.25, incl entry to centre ⏱ 2.15pm Mon, Wed & Fri

Dublin Literary Pub Crawl (2, A3) A night tour of four literary drinking holes, starting at the Duke. The 2¼-hour tour is led by two actors who perform extracts by famous Dublin writers along the way. It's a popular tour so book ahead at Dublin Tourism (5, D3; ☎ 605 7700), or get to the pub by 7pm to secure a ticket.
☎ 670 5602 📖 www .dublinpubcrawl.com ✉ Duke (upstairs), 9 Duke St €️ €10/8 🕑 7.30pm daily & noon Sun Apr-Dec, 7.30pm Thu-Sun Jan-Mar

Dublin Musical Pub Crawl
Two musicians play tunes and explain the evolution of Irish music in Temple Bar pubs, including the Palace Bar and the Norseman. The musicians, drawn from a pool of 25 pros, are all excellent, as is the music. Be sure to arrive early to reserve your ticket.
☎ 475 3313 📖 www .discoverdublin.ie ✉ Oliver St John Gogarty's (5, D2; upstairs), cnr Fleet & Anglesea St €️ €10/8 🕑 7.30pm May-Oct, 7.30pm Fri & Sat Nov & Feb-Apr

Historical Walking Tours
Trinity College history graduates lead this 'seminar on the street', which explores the Potato Famine, Easter Rising, Civil War and Partition. Sights include Trinity (p9), City Hall (p37), Dublin Castle (p20) and Four Courts (p37). In summer, themed tours on architecture, women in Irish history and the birth of the Irish state are also held.
☎ 878 0227 📖 www .historicalinsights.ie ✉ Trinity College, College Green entrance (2, A1) €️ €10/8 🕑 11am, noon & 3pm May-Aug, 11am & 3pm Apr & Sep, noon Fri-Sun Oct-Mar

Spooky
Ghost Walk Macabre
Trapeze Theatre Company runs this excellent tour, which combines theatre performance with a walk through the spooky corners of Georgian Dublin. Sinister writings by Bram Stoker, Oscar Wilde and James Joyce are brilliantly dramatised, as are some of the city's more brutal murders. Bookings essential.
☎ 087-677 1512 ✉ Fusiliers' Arch (6, D3), St Stephen's Green €️ €12/10 🕑 7.30pm

Zozimus Ghostly Experience (5, B3) A 1½-hour tour of Dublin's superstitious and seedy medieval past. The guide — the blind and ageing character Zozimus — recounts stories of murders, great escapes and mythical events. Bookings essential.

☎ 661 8646 📖 www .zozimus.com ✉ Dublin Castle gate, Dame St €️ €10/8.50 🕑 9pm summer; 7pm winter, by arrangement

Train
Railtours Ireland
Virtually every must-see sight in Ireland is accessible on Railtours' half-, full- and three-day trips, which include the Aran Islands, Cliffs of Moher, Ring of Kerry, Connemara and Giant's Causeway. Trips start at and return to Heuston Station (3, D3) or Connolly Station (4, F3). Bookings essential.
☎ 856 0045 📖 www .railtours.ie ✉ Railtours Desk, Dublin Tourism (5, D3) €️ €29-399

Water
Sea Safari
Adrenaline-pumping tours on high-speed boats around the sights of Dublin Bay, including Lambay Island, Killiney Bay and Howth (p39). Trips last an hour, must be booked and you're advised to wear warm clothes.
☎ 806 1626 📖 www .seasafari.ie ✉ Malahide Marina (1, C1) €️ €25/30

On the Rock Trail
Unknown to most visitors, much of Dublin's musical history is found in seemingly innocent — and very uncool — places. The *Rock 'n' Stroll* booklet (€3.20) from Dublin Tourism (5, D3) takes you on a walk past 21 everyday sites made extraordinary because of their musical connections. Stops include the restaurant where Sinead O'Connor waitered, the shoe shop where Ronan Keating worked and the hearing-aid shop whose name Bono nicked.

Shopping

Dubliners might be relatively new to the shopping-as-pastime craze, but they've taken to it with a gusto normally reserved for last-drinks call at the pub. On weekends especially, the main shopping districts are chock-a-block with gaggles of teenagers, pram-pushing families, serious consumer couples, tourists and the odd elderly lady bravely making her way through the chaos.

Unless you enjoy the hustle and bustle, save your shopping for weekdays – the earlier the better.

British and US chains dominate the high street and major shopping centres but there are also numerous small, independent shops selling high-quality, locally made goods. Irish designer clothing and street wear, handmade jewellery, unusual homewares and crafts, and cheeses to die for are readily available if you know where to look.

While souvenir hunters can still buy toy sheep, Guinness magnets and shamrock tea towels, a new breed of craft shop offers one-off or limited-edition crafts and art. Traditional Irish products, such as crystal and knitwear, remain popular choices and you can increasingly find innovative modern takes on the classics.

Almost all shops accept credit cards and you are rarely more than 100m from an ATM in the main shopping districts.

Most shops are open from 9am or 10am to 6pm Monday to Saturday (until 8pm Thursday) and from noon to 6pm Sunday.

Hot Shop Spots

Dublin's main shopping areas are:

Grafton St (6, D1–D3) Boutiques, department stores, clothing and music chains.

West of Grafton St Small, funky independent shops, street wear, designer and second-hand clothing, jewellery shops, cosmetics.

East of Grafton St Antiques and traditional crafts, art galleries.

Temple Bar (5) Record shops, vintage clothes, kooky knick-knacks.

Henry St (4, D4) High-street chains, department stores, sportswear.

Talbot St (4, E4) Bargain-basement clothes, homewares, furnishings and hardware.

Capel St (4, C5) Outdoor gear, car accessories, cheap furniture.

Francis St (4, A6–B7) Antiques.

Two stragglers hurry to catch up with Dublin's latest pastime; shopping

DEPARTMENT STORES & SHOPPING CENTRES

Arnott's (4, D4) Occupying a huge block with entrances on Henry, Liffey and Abbey Sts, a recent overhaul has made this one of Dublin's best department stores. From garden furniture to high fashion, it's all here, and there's a great selection of kids' designer gear on the 1st floor.
☎ 805 0400 ✉ 12 Henry St ⏰ 9am-6.30pm Mon-Sat, to 9pm Thu; noon-6pm Sun 🚆 O'Connell St 🚇 Abbey Street

Brown Thomas (2, A3) Dublin's most exclusive and expensive store has the best cosmetics counters in the city, stylish homewares, bed linen, luggage, electronics and a large selection of Irish crystal. Irish fashion designers represented here include John Rocha, Lainey Keogh, Philip Treacy and Orla Kiely. The 2nd-floor café is small and surprisingly relaxed, as is Brown's Bar in the basement.
☎ 605 6666 ✉ 92 Grafton St ⏰ 9am-6pm Mon-Sat, to 9pm Thu; 10am-6.30pm Sun 🚆 all cross-city 🚇 St Stephen's Green

Dunnes Stores (6, D3) A favourite choice with Irish mothers wanting to outfit the whole family, Dunnes offers everyday men's, women's and children's clothing that mimics current fashion trends at a price that won't break the bank. Their good value homewares department is of the pine-mug-tree and suedette-cushion variety. Look for branches across the city.
☎ 671 4629 ✉ 62 Grafton St ⏰ 9am-6.30pm Mon-Sat, to 9pm Thu; noon-6pm Sun 🚆 all cross-city 🚇 St Stephen's Green

Jervis Centre (4, C4) An ultramodern, domed mall that's a veritable shrine to the British chain store. Boots, Top Shop, Debenhams, Argos, Dixons, M&S, Dorothy Perkins and even Tesco all get a look-in.
☎ 878 1323 ✉ Jervis St ⏰ 9am-6pm Mon-Sat, to 9pm Thu, to 6.30pm Sat; noon-6pm Sun 🚆 Jervis

Penny's (4, D4) Even in new currency this is the place to head for reasonably streetwise knits, T-shirts, bikinis and underwear at prices you won't beat anywhere. OK, so you mightn't clad yourself from head to toe here, but you'll definitely pick up a cute hoodie and tee for under your Evisu denim jacket.
☎ 872 0466 ✉ 37 O'Connell St ⏰ 8.30am-6.30pm Mon-Sat, to 9pm Thu; noon-6pm Sun 🚆 O'Connell St 🚇 Abbey Street

Powerscourt Centre (6, C2) This upmarket shopping mall in an 18th-century town house is where discerning shoppers quietly visit boutiques, beauty salons and the 1st-floor art, craft and antique shops. Karen Millen and fcuk are also here, as is Solomon Gallery, a great vegetarian restaurant and a

Gain strength for more shopping at the Powerscourt Centre

Sales
Dublin has two universally observed sales periods each year: July and January. But you'll find many shops offering discounts between-times on stock they can't move. Dedicated bargain hunters should find Dublin's sales quite satisfying. Reductions can be sizeable (25% to 50% off) and prices are often reduced further (up to 75%) as the weeks wear on.

The minimalist St Stephen's Green shopping centre

wig store. **Mimo** (☎ 679 7789), the courtyard restaurant, is a pleasant spot to gather yourself.
☎ 679 4144 ✉ 59 William St S ⏱ 10am-6pm Mon-Fri, to 8pm Thu; 9am-6pm Sat; noon-6pm Sun 🚌 all cross-city 🚆 St Stephen's Green

Roches Stores (4, C4)
Ditching its traditional bargain-basement image, the recently unveiled new-look Roches is a modern department store at its

shiny best – bold and glass-fronted on the outside and street-smart fashion labels like Zara, Warehouse and G-Star inside, as well as the obligatory homewares and electrical sections.
☎ 873 0044 ✉ 83 Henry St ⏱ 9am-6.30pm Mon-Sat, to 9pm Thu; noon-6pm Sun 🚌 O'Connell St 🚆 Jervis

St Stephen's Green Shopping Centre (6, C3)
A 1980s version of a 19th-century shopping arcade,

the dramatic, balconied interior and central courtyard are a bit too grand for the nondescript chain stores within. There's a Boots, Benetton, TJ Maxx and a Levi's shop, as well as a Dunnes Store with supermarket.
☎ 478 0888 ✉ cnr King St S & St Stephen's Green W ⏱ 9am-6pm Mon-Sat, to 9pm Thu; noon-6pm Sun 🚌 all cross-city 🚆 St Stephen's Green

Westbury Mall (6, D2)
Wedged between the five-star Westbury Hotel and the expensive jewellery stores of Johnson's Ct, this small mall has a handful of pricey, specialist shops, some of which are thriving on their reputation; others are struggling with the slow passing trade.
✉ Clarendon St ⏱ 10am-6pm Mon-Sat, 12-5pm Sun 🚌 all cross-city 🚆 St Stephen's Green

HIGH-END FASHION

Alias Tom (6, D2) Dublin's best designer menswear store, where friendly staff guide you through casuals by bling Burberry, and YSL Rive Gauche. Downstairs it's classic tailored suits and Patrick Cox shoes.
☎ 671 5443 ✉ Duke Lane ⏱ 9.30am-6pm Mon-Sat, to 8pm Thu 🚌 all cross-city 🚆 St Stephen's Green

Allicano (6, D2) Silky, di-aphanous, dressy outfits for lithe-figured style queens from a crop of young,

innovative Belgian, French, Danish and Irish designers, including Dubliner Una O'Reilly.
☎ 677 3430 ✉ 4 Johnsons Pl ⏱ 10am-6pm Mon-Sat, to 7pm Thu 🚌 all cross-city 🚆 St Stephen's Green

Claire Garvey (5, A3)
This den of purples, golds and swirling paint is the perfect setting for the theatrical collection of Claire Garvey. The elf-like designer, who studied costume-making in Mos-

cow, creates one-off pieces with hand-ruched silks, velvets, feathers, quilting, sequins and rosettes. The ultimate statement for the cashed-up extrovert.
☎ 671 7287 ✉ 6 The Music Hall, Cow's Lane, Temple Bar ⏱ 10am-5.30pm Tue-Sat, to 7pm Thu 🚌 all cross-city 🚆 Jervis

Costume (6, C2) From casuals to sparkly full-length dresses, Costume specialises in offbeat women's wear from mainly

Passion for Fashion

After years in the wilderness, Irish designers are making a name for themselves on the international fashion stage. John Rocha, whose own-label clothes have been high fashion for the past decade, has branched into hotel design (Morrison, p99) and homewares, as has classic womenswear designer Louise Kennedy (Waterford Crystal). Both Orla Kiely's and Lulu Guinness' funky bags are a hit in London and New York, while Philip Treacy makes wild theatrical hats for international clients and the catwalk. Lainey Keogh's weathered, shorn and torn knitwear has graced the lithe bodies of supermodels and even Madonna.

young Irish designers. Their own Costume label sits alongside pieces by Pauric Sweeny and Antonia Campbell-Hughes, while Anna Sui and small Italian and French labels make up the foreign contingent.
☎ 679 4188 ✉ 10 Castle Market ✆ 10am-6pm Mon-Sat, to 7pm Thu 🚌 all cross-city 🚇 St Stephen's Green

Design Centre Dedicated to Irish-only designer women's wear, with well-made, conservative outfits, including suits, evening wear and knitwear. Labels include Louise Kennedy, John Rocha, Mairead Whisker and Marc O'Neill.
☎ 679 5718 ✉ Powerscourt Centre (6, C2) ✆ 10am-6pm Mon-Fri, to 8pm Thu; 9.30am-6pm Sat 🚌 all cross-city 🚇 St Stephen's Green

Louis Copeland (5, A1) A Dublin tradition for off-the-peg suits and casual menswear, with Lacoste, Burberry, Dior and Louis Ferraud. Louis himself works at the original Capel St store; the others are at 29-30 Pembroke St Lower (4, E8) and 18-19 Wicklow St (6, D1).

☎ 872 1600 ✉ 39-41 Capel St ✆ 9am-5.30pm Mon-Sat, to 7.30pm Thu 🚌 37, 70, 134, 172 🚇 Jervis

Smock (5, A3) This tiny designer shop on the edge of Temple Bar sells cutting-edge international women's wear from classy 'investment labels' Easton Pearson, Veronique Branquinho and AF Vandevorft, as well as a small range of interesting jewellery and lingerie.
☎ 613 9000 ✉ Smock Alley Ct, West Essex St

✆ 10.30am-6pm Mon-Fri, 10am-6pm Sat 🚌 all cross-city

Tulle (6, C2) Australian designers with attitude Sass and Bide and Wheels & Doll Baby, plus Euro designers Fornarina and Sonia Rykiel, are stocked in this small outlet for fashion-savvied young gals, tucked away in the arcade.
☎ 679 9115 ✉ 28 George's Street Arcade ✆ 10am-6pm Mon-Sat, to 8pm Thu 🚌 all cross-city 🚇 St Stephen's Green

"Hmm, dinner at Halo (p68) or this fab dress from Smock?"

STREET WEAR

Aspecto (6, D2) Boys who like their style with a side serving of attitude should head to this UK store, stocked with Duffer, Evisu, Carhartt and Paul Smith casuals, along with some nifty shoes by the likes of Camper, Vans and Timberland.
☎ 671 9302 ✉ 6 Anne St S 🕐 10am-6pm Mon-Sat, to 8pm Thu; 1-6pm Sun 🚌 all cross-city 🚇 St Stephen's Green

BT2 (6, D2) Brown Thomas' young and funky offshoot, with expensive casuals for men and women and a branch of Nude juice bar upstairs overlooking Grafton St. Brands include DKNY, Diesel, Ted Baker and Tommy Hilfiger.
☎ 679 5666 ✉ 88 Grafton St 🕐 9am-6.30pm Mon-Sat, to 9pm Thu, to 7pm Sat; 10am-6.30pm Sun 🚌 all cross-city 🚇 St Stephen's Green

Flip (5, C3) This hip Irish label takes the best male fashion moods of the 1950s and serves them back to us, minus the mothball smell. US college shirts, logo T-shirts, Oriental and Hawaiian shirts, Fonz-style leather jackets and well-cut jeans mix it with the genuine second-hand gear upstairs.
☎ 671 4299 ✉ 4 Fownes St 🕐 10am-6pm Mon-Sat, to 7pm Thu & Sat; 1.30-6pm Sun 🚌 all cross-city 🚇 St Stephen's Green

Foundation (5, D3) This Irish-owned label is stocked with funky clobber for young bucks on the make and girls who prefer understated cool to glitzy glam. Labels include Boxfresh, Mambo, Fred Perry and Yo Japan.
☎ 670 4869 ✉ 6-9 Trinity St 🕐 9.30am-6pm Mon-Sat, to 8pm Thu; noon-6pm Sun 🚌 all cross-city 🚇 St Stephen's Green

You'll flip for Flip's clothes

Urban Outfitters (5, C2) Funky street wear and labels mix with gadgets and homewares at this branch of the US chain. As the DJ spins tunes from the record outlet, boys browse G-Star denims, Pringle knits and Fiorucci trousers, while girls choose between Claudie Pierlot, W&LT and Mandarina Duck.
☎ 670 6202 ✉ 7 Fownes St 🕐 10am-7pm Mon-Sat, to 8pm Thu & Sat; 11am-6pm Sun 🚌 all cross-city 🚇 Jervis

CLOTHING & SHOE SIZES

Women's Clothing

Aust/UK	8	10	12	14	16	18
Europe	36	38	40	42	44	46
Japan	5	7	9	11	13	15
USA	6	8	10	12	14	16

Women's Shoes

Aust/USA	5	6	7	8	9	10
Europe	35	36	37	38	39	40
France only	35	36	38	39	40	42
Japan	22	23	24	25	26	27
UK	3½	4½	5½	6½	7½	8½

Men's Clothing

Aust	92	96	100	104	108	112
Europe	46	48	50	52	54	56

Japan	S	M	M		L	
UK/USA	35	36	37	38	39	40

Men's Shirts (Collar Sizes)

Aust/Japan	38	39	40	41	42	43
Europe	38	39	40	41	42	43
UK/USA	15	15½	16	16½	17	17½

Men's Shoes

Aust/ UK	7	8	9	10	11	12
Europe	41	42	43	44½	46	47
Japan	26	27	27.5	28	29	30
USA	7½	8½	9½	10½	11½	12½

Measurements approximate only; try before you buy.

JEWELLERY

Angles You won't find Claddagh rings or charm bracelets here, just cabinets full of handmade, modern Irish jewellery, most of it by up-and-coming Dublin craftspeople. Commissions are taken and can be sent on to you abroad.
☎ 679 1964 ✉ Westbury Mall (6, D2), Johnson's Ct ⊕ 10am-6pm Mon-Sat, to 7pm Thu 🚌 all cross-city 🚇 St Stephen's Green

Appleby (2, A3) Renowned for the high quality of its gold and silver jewellery, which tends towards more conventional designs, this is the place to shop for serious stuff – diamond rings, sapphire-encrusted cufflinks and Raymond Weil watches.
☎ 679 9572 ✉ 5-6 Johnson's Ct ⊕ 9.30am-5.30pm Mon-Sat, to 7pm Thu, to 6pm Sat 🚌 all cross-city 🚇 St Stephen's Green

Barry Doyle Design Jewellers (6, C2) Upstairs on the southern side of George's St Arcade, Barry Doyle works away in his light-filled, wooden studio producing beautiful, bold, handmade necklaces, bracelets and rings in Celtic and modern designs. Individual pieces can be commissioned – prices are steep but the work is of excellent quality.
☎ 671 2838 ✉ George's St Arcade ⊕ 9am-6pm Mon-Sat, to 8pm Thu 🚌 all cross-city 🚇 St Stephen's Green

Rhinestones (5, D3) Exceptionally fine antique and quirky costume jewellery from the 1920s to 1970s, with pieces priced from €15 to €1500. Victorian jet, 1950s enamel, Art-Deco turquoise, 1930s mother-of-pearl, cut-glass and rhinestone necklaces, bracelets, brooches and rings are displayed by colour in old-fashioned cabinets.
☎ 679 0759 ✉ 18 St Andrew's St ⊕ 9am-6.30pm Mon-Sat, to 8pm Thu; noon-6pm Sun 🚌 all cross-city

Vivien Walsh (5, B2) One of Ireland's best-known jewellery designers, Vivien Walsh uses Swarovski crystal, glass, feathers, pearls and beads to create delicate, fantastical pieces that hark back to the 1920s and beyond. The elaborate necklaces, in vivid turquoise, pink, purple and green, are quite an investment, but simple bracelets can be had for under €30. French and Italian leather bags and shoes complement the displays.
☎ 475 5031 ✉ 24 Stephen St Lower ⊕ 11am-6pm Mon-Fri, to 7pm Thu; 10am-6pm Sat 🚌 all cross-city 🚇 St Stephen's Green

Weir & Sons (2, A3) The largest jeweller in Ireland, this huge store on Grafton St first opened in 1869 and still has its original wooden cabinets and a workshop on the premises. There's new and antique Irish jewellery (including Celtic designs) and a huge selection of watches, Irish crystal, porcelain, leather and travel goods.
☎ 677 9678 ✉ 96-99 Grafton St ⊕ 9am-5.30pm Mon-Sat, to 8pm Thu 🚌 all cross-city

Consumer R&R
There's no need to shop till you drop while pounding the streets of Dublin. Several stores have quiet and comfortable cafés where you can refuel, take stock and plan your next move. These include:
Avoca Handweavers (p61)
Brown Thomas (p54)
BT2 (p57)
Kilkenny (p61)
Powerscourt Centre (p54)
Winding Stair (p65)

RETRO STORES

Eager Beaver (5, C2) In a creaky wooden building that looks even older than the fashions, Beaver provides racks of no-nonsense, second-hand gear. There are cords, Levi's, combats, golf slacks, leathers, army jackets, wedding suits and a huge range of Hawaiian shirts. ☎ 677 3342 ✉ 17 Crown Alley 🕐 9.30am-6pm Mon-Sat, to 7.30pm Thu & Fri; noon-6pm Sun 🚌 all cross-city 🚊 Jervis

Harlequin (6, C2) Harlequin stocks some exquisite vintage gems as well as the standard second-hand jeans, T-shirts, shoes, bags and suits. ☎ 671 0202 ✉ 13 Castle Market 🕐 10.30am-6pm Mon-Sat, to 7pm Thu 🚌 all cross-city 🚊 St Stephen's Green

Jenny Vander (6, C2) More *Breakfast at Tiffany's* chic than the castoffs from *Hair,* this second-hand store oozes elegance and sophistication. Exquisite beaded handbags, fur-trimmed coats, richly patterned dresses and costume jewellery priced as if it were the real thing are snapped up by discerning fashionistas looking for something quirky to wear with their Marc Jacobs suits. ☎ 677 0406 ✉ 50 Drury St 🕐 10am-5.45pm Mon-Sat 🚌 all cross-city 🚊 St Stephen's Green

A Store is Born (6, C2) Discretely hidden for six days a week behind a garage roller-door, this store opens up on Saturdays to reveal a bounty of paisley dresses, peasant tops, belts, beads, cashmere cardies, sequined singlets, wide-collared men's shirts and suit pants. ☎ 679 5866 ✉ 34 Clarendon St 🕐 10am-6pm Sat 🚌 all cross-city 🚊 St Stephen's Green

Wild Child (6, B2) If you're in the market for a groovy pair of Crimplene flares and a bright tangerine body shirt, then this is the place to head to. You'll find good quality men's and women's clothing from the '60s, '70s and '80, supplemented by new retro-style jewellery and glittery, glam nail polish. ☎ 475 5099 ✉ 61 Great George's St S 🕐 10am-6pm Mon-Sat, to 7pm Thu; 1-6pm Sun 🚌 16, 16a, 16c, 19, 19a, 65, 83 🚊 St Stephen's Green

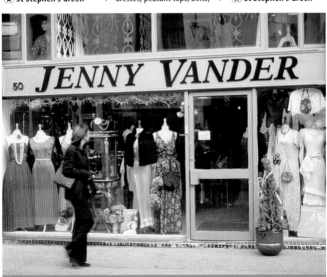

Find clothes for your inner Holly Golightly at Jenny Vander

MARKETS

Blackrock Market The long-running Blackrock Market in an old merchant house and yard in this seaside village has all manner of stalls selling everything from New Age crystals and dodgy Dollar albums to futons and piping-hot French waffles.
✉ Main St, Blackrock (1, C1) ⏱ 11am-5.30pm Sat, from 10am Sun
🚆 Blackrock

Cow's Lane Market (5, A3) Now here's a real market for hipsters. Located in the old Dublin Viking Adventure Centre, this new market brings together over 60 of the best clothing, accessory and craft stalls in town. Buy cutting-edge designer duds from the likes of Suki & Nic, punky T-shirts, retro handbags, costume jewellery and even clubby baby wear.
✉ Cow's Lane, Temple Bar ⏱ 10am-5pm Sat
🚌 all cross-city 🚆 Jervis

George's Street Arcade (6, C2) Dublin's best nonfood market (there's sadly not much competition) is sheltered within an elegant Victorian Gothic arcade. Apart from shops and stalls selling new and old clothes, second-hand books, hats, posters, jewellery and records, there's a fortune teller, some gourmet nibbles and a fish and chipper who does a roaring trade.
✉ btwn Great George's St S & Drury St ⏱ 10am-6pm Mon-Sat
🚌 all cross-city

Meeting House Square Market One of the best places to spend Saturday morning, this market buzzes with visitors and locals stocking up on organic, gourmet and imported exotica. Munch on sushi, paella, waffles, crepes and sizzling sausages, while perusing stalls of farmhouse cheeses, hand-pressed juices, organic meats and tubs of garlic pesto.
✉ Meeting House Sq (5, B2) ⏱ 9am-5pm Sat
🚌 all cross-city 🚆 Jervis

Moore St Market (4, C4) An open-air, steadfastly 'Old Dublin' market, with fruit, fish and flowers. Vendors hawk cheap cigarettes, tobacco and chocolate. Don't try to buy just one banana though – if it says 10 for €1, that's what it is.
✉ Moore St ⏱ 9am-4pm Mon-Sat 🚌 all cross-city 🚆 Jervis

Find out what all the fuss is about; pick up a copy of *Ulysses* at the George's Street Arcade

ARTS & CRAFTS

As well as mass-produced tourist fodder, a great number of Dublin shops now specialise in high-end crafts made by local artisans. If fine art is what you're after, try the commercial galleries (p31).

Avoca Handweavers (2, A2) Combining clothing, homewares, a basement food hall and an excellent top-floor café (p72), Avoca promotes a stylish but homey brand of modern Irish life. Many of the garments are woven, knitted and naturally dyed at their Wicklow factory. The children's section, with unusual knits, fairy outfits, bee-covered gumboots and dinky toys, is fantastic. ☎ 677 4215 ✉ 11-13 Suffolk St ☉ 10am-6pm Mon-Sat, to 8pm Thu; 11am-6pm Sun 🚌 all cross-city

Bridge (4, B5) Housed in a Georgian terrace on the quays, this place is part art gallery, part high-end crafts store. Regular exhibitions are held out the back, while the shop sells paintings, ceramics, woodcarvings and jewellery. ☎ 872 9702 ✉ 6 Ormond Quay Upper ☉ 10am-6pm Mon-Sat, 2-5pm Sun 🚌 all cross-city 🚇 Four Courts

Decor (4, C8) Decor is like your granny's attic, with far funkier contents. The place is crammed with chunky teak and mahogany furniture from Southeast Asia, basalt buddha statues, off-beat gilded mirrors and exotic throws coming out the doors – and all at a price we like, to boot.

And when they dust off her JFK calendar and SodaStream, we'll be there. ☎ 475 9010 ✉ 14a Wexford St ☉ 10am-6pm Mon-Sat 🚌 16, 16a, 16c, 19, 19a, 65, 83 🚇 St Stephen's Green

Dublin City Gallery – The Hugh Lane Shop (4, C3) You could waste some wonderful time in this almost secret place, digging out cubist fridge magnets, huge Po-Mo hanging mobiles, masterpiece colour-by-number prints, cloth puppets, unusual wooden toys and beautiful art and pop culture hardbacks. A cultural playground for adults. ☎ 874 1903 ✉ Charlemont House, Parnell Sq N ☉ 9.30am-5pm Tue-Sat, to 6pm Tue-Thu, 11am-5pm Sun 🚌 3, 10, 16, 19, 123 🚇 Connolly Station

Dublin Woollen Mills (5, C1) At the northern end of the Ha'penny Bridge, this is one of Dublin's major

wool outlets. It has a large selection of sweaters, cardigans, scarves, rugs, shawls and other woollen goods and runs a tax-free shopping scheme. ☎ 677 5014 ✉ 41 Ormond Quay Lower ☉ 9.30am-6pm Mon-Sat, to 7.30pm Thu; 1-6pm Sun 🚌 all cross-city 🚇 Jervis

Inreda (4, C8) Inreda is a virtual shrine for Scandinavian design enthusiasts to revere beautifully-crafted modern furniture by Swedese and David Design as well as lighting, ceramics, glassware and accessories by Design House Stockholm. It's pricey stuff but there's no harm in looking, right? ☎ 478 0362 ✉ 71 Camden St Lower ☉ 10.30am-6pm Mon-Fri, 11am-6pm Sat 🚌 16, 16a, 19, 19a, 65, 83

Kilkenny (2, C3) Contemporary, innovative takes on classic Irish crafts, including multicoloured,

Irish Crystal
Once a prized item in the dining room cabinets of grandmothers across the Western world, Irish crystal has undergone something of an overhaul in recent years. While the traditional designs are still available, Irish designer John Rocha has created some sleek, contemporary styles for Waterford Crystal that would never look right resting on a doily. Minimalist, angular and – dare we say it – funky, this is glass with pure class.

modern Irish knits, designer clothing, Orla Kiely bags and some lovely silver jewellery. The glassware and pottery is beautiful and sourced from workshops around the country. A great source for presents.
☎ 677 7066 ✉ 5-6 Nassau St ☾ 8.30am-6pm Mon-Fri, to 8pm Thu; 9am-6pm Sat; 11am-6pm Sun 🚌 all cross-city

Tower Craft Design Centre (3, G4) Buy crafts direct from the artist at these studios

opposite the Waterways Visitor Centre. Around 20 artisans produce jewellery, ceramics, textiles, rugs and leather goods on site. Good bets are Fine Design and Linda Oman jewellery.
☎ 677 5655 ✉ Pearse St (enter via Grand Canal Quay) ☾ 9am-5.30pm Mon-Fri 🚌 1, 2, 3 🚇 Grand Canal Dock, Pearse Station

Whichcraft (6, A1)
A high-end, craft-as-art shop where everything you see

is one-off and handmade in Ireland. They also recently took over the gorgeous contemporary jewellery stock from the sadly defunct DesignYard, which show-cased young international designers. Another branch (☎ 670 9371), with less exclusive gear, is around the corner at 5 Castle Gate, Lord Edward St (6, A1).
☎ 474 1011 ✉ Cow's Lane ☾ 9.30am-6.30pm Mon-Fri, to 8pm Thu; 9am-6.30pm Sat; 10am-6pm Sun 🚌 all cross-city

ANTIQUES

Dublin's antique dealers tend to stick together, making browsing all the more easy. Most reside in Francis St (4, A6–B7) in the Liberties. Other areas include Anne St S (6, D2) or Johnson's Ct (6, D2) for silverware and jewellery, or the antiques gallery on the 1st floor of the Powerscourt Centre (p54). Every second Sunday, Newman House (p38) hosts an antiques and collectibles fair from 11am to 6pm.

Fleury Antiques (4, B7)
Fleury specialises in oil paintings, vases, candelabras, silverware, porcelain and decorative pieces from the 18th century to the 1930s.
☎ 473 0878 ✉ 57 Francis St ☾ 9.30am-6pm Mon-Sat 🚌 49, 50, 56A, 77, 121

H Danker (6, D2) Chock-full of exquisite treasures, this shop specialises in Irish and English antique silver,

jewellery and *objets d'art*.
☎ 677 4009 ✉ 10 Anne St S ☾ 9.30am-6pm Mon-Sat 🚌 all cross-city

Michael Connell Antiques (4, B7) You'll find a huge range of antique light fittings at this antique shop. There's also Edwardian furniture, silver, brassware and china here.
☎ 473 3898 ✉ 53 Francis St ☾ 9.30am-5.30pm Mon-Sat 🚌 49, 50, 56A, 77, 121

Neptune Gallery (6, C2)
Climb the rickety stairs over Busyfeet Café into this Aladdin's Cave of cartography. Pick up dusty maps and prints of Ireland dating from 1600 to 1880 for anything from a few quid up to about €1000.
☎ 671 5021 ✉ 1st fl, 41 William St S ☾ 10am-5.30pm Mon-Fri, 10am-1pm Sat 🚌 all cross-city

Sean Eacrett (4, B7)
This spot offers paintings, prints, *objets d'art* and trinkets as well as functional furniture from the Regency, William IV and Victorian periods.
☎ 454 9467 ✉ 58 Francis St ☾ 9.30am-5.30pm Mon-Sat 🚌 49, 50, 56A, 77, 121

Any Old Iron?
You know the saying. One man's junk, etc. If it's copper piping, Art-Deco taps or even a baptismal font for your bathroom, you'll probably stumble across it in one of the great architectural salvage outlets around the city. Scan the Golden Pages for details.

MUSIC

Claddagh Records (5, C2)
An intimate, well-loved shop with knowledgeable staff, Claddagh specialises in folk, traditional and ethnic music from Ireland, the USA and South America.
☎ 677 0262 ✉ 2 Cecilia St ⌚ 10.30am-5.30pm Mon-Fri, from noon Sat 🚌 all cross-city 🚇 Jervis

Rhythm Records (5, D1)
This grungy little store on the quays has a large U2 section, including major releases, singles, special tour editions, remix albums and suspicious-looking cassettes with photocopied covers. Also posters, videos, postcards and a 7-inch collection from rock and popsters.
☎ 671 9594 ✉ 1 Aston Quay ⌚ 11am-6pm Mon-Sat 🚌 all cross-city 🚇 Abbey Street

Tower Records (2, A3)
You'll find a broad selection of CDs, records and DVDs here, from the latest mainstream releases to good alternative rock, jazz, soul and classical sounds.
☎ 671 3250 ✉ 16 Wicklow St ⌚ 9am-9pm Mon-Sat, 11.30am-7.30pm Sun 🚌 all cross-city

Walton's (6, B1)
These traditional Irish music specialists sell CDs, instruments (such as banjos, bodhráns, guitars), sheet music for Irish harp, flute and fiddle, and song books featuring tunes by Irish music greats, including the Wolfe Tones, the Fureys and the Dubliners. You can also take two-hour crash courses in the bodhrán or tin whistle at their music school.
☎ 475 0661 ✉ 69-70 Great George's St S ⌚ 9am-6pm Mon-Sat, noon-5pm Sun 🚌 16, 16a, 19, 19a, 65, 83

FOOD & DRINK

Bretzel Bakery (4, C9)
The bagels might be a bit on the chewy side, but they've got their charms – as do the scrumptious selections of breads, savoury snacks, cakes and biscuits that have locals queuing out the door on weekends. Recertified as kosher since 2003, the bakery has been on this Portobello site since 1870.
☎ 475 2724 ✉ 1a Lennox St ⌚ 8.30am-3pm Mon-Fri, to 6pm Tue, Wed & Fri, to 7pm Thu; 9am-5pm Sat; 9am-1pm Sun 🚌 14, 15, 65, 83

Magills (6, D2) With its characterful old facade and tiny dark interior, Magills' old-world charm reminds you how Clarendon St must have once looked. Family-run, you get the distinct feeling that every Irish and French cheese, olive oil, packet of Italian pasta and salami was hand-picked.
☎ 671 3830 ✉ 14 Clarendon St ⌚ 9.30am-5.45pm Mon-Sat 🚌 all cross-city 🚇 St Stephen's Green

Mitchell & Son Wine Merchants (6, E3)
Established in 1805, the store is still run by a sixth and seventh generation Mitchell father-and-son team. Wines, champagnes, Irish whiskey and Cuban cigars fill the cavernous space. You can also buy stylish wine racks, glasses, hip flasks and ice buckets.
☎ 676 0766 ✉ 21 Kildare St ⌚ 9am-5.30pm Mon-Fri, from 10.30am Sat 🚌 11, 11a, 14, 14a, 15a 🚇 St Stephen's Green

The big cheese, Sheridan's cheesemongers (p64)

Sheridans Cheesemongers (6, D2) If heaven were a cheese shop, this would be it. Wooden shelves are laden with rounds of farmhouse cheeses, sourced from around the country by Kevin and Seamus Sheridan who have almost single-handedly revived cheese-making in Ireland. You can taste any one of the 60 cheeses on display and pick up some wild Irish salmon, Italian pastas and olives while you're at it. ☎ 679 3143 ✉ 11 Anne St S ⏱ 10am-6pm Mon-Fri, from 9.30am Sat 🚌 all cross-city 🚇 St Stephen's Green

BOOKS

Cathach Books (2, A3) Rare editions of Irish literature and history, including works by Wilde, Joyce, Yeats and Beckett, and a large selection of signed first editions in one of Dublin's best antiquarian bookshops. ☎ 671 8676 ✉ 10 Duke St ⏱ 9.30am-5.45pm Mon-Sat 🚌 all cross-city

Eason's (4, D4) You'll find mostly mainstream popular fiction in this massive shop, but on the other hand, it's the largest stockist of magazines and international newspapers. ☎ 873 3811 ✉ 40 O'Connell St Lower ⏱ 8.30am-6.45pm Mon-Sat, to 8.45pm Thu, to 7.45pm Fri; 12.45-5.45pm Sun 🚌 all cross-city 🚇 Abbey

Forbidden Planet (5, D1) Science fiction and fantasy specialist, with books, videos, comics, magazines, figurines and posters. Just the place for those Dr Spock ears or a *Star Wars* light sabre. ☎ 671 0688 ✉ 5-6 Crampton Quay ⏱ 10am-6pm Mon-Sat, to 7pm Thu; noon-5pm Sun 🚌 all cross-city 🚇 Abbey Street

Winding Stair

Murder Ink (6, E2) All manner of murder mystery and crime novels are in this small specialist bookstore that has categorisation down to a fine art — choose from historical mystery, romantic crime, sci-fi mystery, true crime and more. ☎ 677 7570 ✉ 15 Dawson St ⏱ 10am-5.30pm Mon-Sat, noon-5pm Sun 🚌 all cross-city 🚇 St Stephen's Green

Waterstone's (2, B3) Although it is large and multistoried, Waterstone's somehow manages to maintain that snugly, hide-in-a-corner ambience that book lovers adore. The broad selection of books is supplemented by five bookcases of Irish fiction, as well as poetry, drama, politics

Dublin Reads
Add the following Dublin-based books to those by Joyce (*Ulysses, Dubliners, Finnegans Wake*) and Roddy Doyle (*The Commitments, The Snapper, The Van, Paddy Clarke, Ha Ha Ha*):
- *Butcher Boy* – Patrick McCabe
- *Down all the Days* – Christy Brown
- *The Ginger Man* – JP Donleavy
- *The Journey Home* – Dermot Bolger
- *The Parts* – Keith Ridgway
- *The Quare Fellow* – Brendan Behan

and history. Book-signings every Thursday evening; check board outside for details.
☎ 679 1415 ✉ 7 Dawson St ⏱ 9am-7pm Mon-Fri, to 8pm Thu; 9am-6.30pm Sat; noon-6pm Sun 🚌 all cross-city

Winding Stair (5, C1) This is a creaky old place that is just oozing with character. It can be some effort to manoeuvre yourself past the bookish types through to the heaving bookcases crammed with new and second-hand

books. When you've had enough of book browsing, head up the winding stairs to the excellent café (p69).
☎ 873 3292 ✉ 40 Ormond Quay Lower ⏱ 9.30am-6pm Mon-Sat 🚌 all cross-city 🚃 Jervis

FOR CHILDREN

Baby Bambino (6, C2) If you can afford the fabulously flamboyant designer gear in this shop, then let the kids go wild. Choose from funky leather jackets, cowboy boots, fake furs, ponchos, fake leopard skin shoes and more from DKNY, D&G, Joseph, Katherine Hamnett and Gianfranco Ferre. Girls from 0 to 16 years, boys 0 to 10 years.
☎ 671 1590 ✉ 41 Clarendon St ⏱ 10am-6pm Mon-Sat, to 7pm Thu 🚌 all cross-city 🚃 St Stephen's Green

Early Learning Centre (4, C4) Fun with an educational bent for the tiniest tots, including ELC-brand plastic and wooden toys, spelling and numerical games, simple devices that honk and squeak and a good range of Thomas the Tank Engine stuff.
☎ 873 1945 ✉ 3 Henry St ⏱ 9am-5pm Mon-Sat, to 8pm Thu, to 5.30pm Sat; 1-5pm Sun 🚌 all cross-city 🚃 Jervis

Gymboree (6, D2) Good-quality, own-brand clothes for boys and girls aged one to seven from this US chain store. The

big TV screening children's programmes at the back of the shop is the perfect place to deposit little tantrum-throwers while you look around.
☎ 670 3331 ✉ 75 Grafton St ⏱ 10am-6pm Mon-Sat, to 8pm Thu; noon-6pm Sun 🚌 all cross-city 🚃 St Stephen's Green

Mothercare The ground floor of this British chain stocks good quality, own-label baby clothes, shoes, toys, books and sleepwear, while upstairs are cots and bedding, highchairs and maternity wear. There's another branch (☎ 878 1184) in the Jervis Centre (p54).
☎ 478 4755 ✉ St Stephen's Green Shopping Centre (6, C3) ⏱ 9.30am-6pm Mon-Sat, to 8pm Thu; noon-6pm Sun 🚌 all cross-city 🚃 St Stephen's Green

Rainbow Crafts This small but well-stocked toy shop stocks a fun array of puppets, educational aids, wooden and tin toys, traditional Irish dolls, doll's houses and furniture, kites, puzzles and a big range of rubber stamps.

☎ 677 7632 ✉ Westbury Mall (6, D2) ⏱ 10am-6pm Mon-Fri, to 7pm Thu; 9am-6pm Sat 🚌 all cross-city 🚃 St Stephen's Green

Smyths Toys (4, C4) Toy superstore, with towering aisles full of Barbies, Lego, various action men, soft toys, puzzles, board games and a whole room devoted to Playstations, Gameboys and videos.
☎ 878 2878 ✉ Jervis St ⏱ 10am-6pm Mon-Sat, to 9pm Thu; 1-6pm Sun 🚌 all cross-city 🚃 Jervis

Smyths Toys, take the kids if you dare

SPECIALIST SHOPS

Blue Eriu (6, C1) In a fantastic, otherworldly, white space, Blue Eriu sells top-end skincare, cosmetics and haircare from the likes of Prada, Shu Uemura and Kleins, as well as scented candles, oils and artisan perfumes. Their facials and massages are pricey but highly regarded.
☎ 672 5776 ⊠ 7 William St S ⏱ 10am-6pm Mon-Sat, to 8pm Mon-Thu 🚌 all cross-city

Decent Cigar Emporium (6, D3) When the buzz of Grafton St gets too much, slip up this discreet staircase, recline in a plush leather armchair and run your nose along a sweet hand-rolled, long-filler cigar. With the smoking ban in place you'll have to wait until you get home to light up but a glass of red wine and a cup of Illy coffee later, you'll barely remember your urge, or the clamour below.
☎ 671 6451 ⊠ 46 Grafton St ⏱ 10am-6pm Mon-Sat, to 8pm Thu; 1.30-5.30pm Sun 🚌 all city-centre 🚇 St Stephen's Green

Great Outdoors (6, D2) Dublin's best outdoors store, with gear for hiking, camping, surfing, mountaineering, swimming and more. Fleeces, tents, inflatable dinghies, boots and gas cookers – they're all here.
☎ 679 4293 ⊠ 20 Chatham St ⏱ 9.30am-5.30pm Mon-Sat, to 8pm Thu 🚌 all cross-city 🚇 St Stephen's Green

Haus (5, C3) Cutting-edge designer furniture and homewares from the drawing boards of the big names, such as Phillipe Starck, Le Corbusier and our own Eileen Gray.
☎ 679 5155 ⊠ 3-4 Crow St ⏱ 9am-6pm Mon-Fri, from 10am Sat 🚌 all cross-city

Irish Historical Picture Company (5, B1) With a print collection that's second only to the holdings at the National Library, this place is jammed full with more than 12,000 pictures taken around Ireland at the turn of the 20th century. The prints cover all 32 counties and range from town streetscapes to images of bog cutters. Mounted prints can be framed within minutes.
☎ 872 0144 ⊠ 5 Ormond Quay Lower ⏱ 9am-6pm Mon-Fri, 10am-5pm Sat & Sun 🚌 all cross-city 🚇 Jervis

Knobs and Knockers (2, B3) Despite the saucy name, this shop in fact offers a rather sober selection of reproduction Georgian door knockers, knobs, handles and locks. Here's where you get that Dublinesque lion's-head knocker you've always dreamed of. They also sell model sailing ships and *pétanque* sets.
☎ 671 0288 ⊠ 19 Nassau St ⏱ 9.30am-5.30pm Mon-Sat, to 8pm Thu 🚌 all cross-city

Out of the Blue Eriu

Natural Shoe Store (6, C2) Give your feet a treat at this tiny, spartan shop that specialises in natural, comfortable shoes. Apart from therapeutic but cool Birkenstocks and Komodos, there are 'vegetarian' shoes and handmade shoes in two designs by a shoemaker in Cork.
☎ 671 4978 ⊠ 25 Drury St ⏱ 9am-5.30pm Mon-Sat 🚌 all cross-city 🚇 St Stephen's Green

Optica (6, D2) Who says guys don't make passes at girls who wear glasses? Knock 'em dead in head-turning specs and shades by Chanel, D&G, Stella McCartney and Oliver Peoples.
☎ 677 4705 ⊠ 1 Royal Hibernian Way ⏱ 9.30am-5.30pm Mon-Sat, to 6.30pm Thu 🚌 all cross-city 🚇 St Stephen's Green

Eating

Dublin's food and restaurant scene is finally moving with the times, spurred on by local passion for dining out and the demands of foreign visitors. You can now eat anything from French *haute cuisine* to Nepalese and pretty much everything in between. But while there's been much talk of the culinary revolution sweeping the city, most of the flag-waving is being done by the pricey gastronomic restaurants. Finding a decent mid-range meal, at a price you can stomach, can still be a difficult task.

The most concentrated restaurant area is **Temple Bar**, but apart from a handful of good places, the bulk of eateries offer bland, unimaginative fodder and cheap set menus for tourists. Better food and service can usually be found around **Grafton St**, while the top-end restaurants are clustered around **Merrion Sq** and **Fitzwilliam Sq**. Fast-food chains dominate the **northside**, though some fine cafés and eateries are thankfully appearing there too.

Ireland has excellent beef, pork, seafood, dairy foods and winter vegetables, and many good restaurants now source their ingredients locally, from organic and artisan producers.

For many restaurants, particularly those in Temple Bar, it's worth booking for Friday or Saturday nights to ensure a table.

Meal Costs

The pricing symbols used in this chapter indicate the average cost of a main course at dinner, or other peak times.

€	under €8
€ €	€8–15
€ € €	€16–25
€ € € €	over €25

No Smoke Without Ire

Since the smoking ban in all public places took effect at the end of March 2004, those who once enjoyed a postprandial toke at the table must now – rain or shine – satisfy their nicotine hit outdoors. Best bet for smokers is to find a restaurant with a terrace or buy an umbrella.

Try a little bit of this and a little bit of that at the Epicurean Food Hall (p68)

NORTH OF THE LIFFEY

101 Talbot
(4, E4) € €
Mediterranean/Middle Eastern
101 Talbot is a funky little restaurant with brightly painted walls, wooden floorboards and check tablecloths. The eclectic menu, which changes daily, may feature their home-made pork, sage and apricot sausage with red-onion relish starter – if you're lucky – it's a firm favourite of ours.
☎ 874 5011 ✉ 101 Talbot St ☺ 5-11pm Tue-Sat 🚆 all cross-city 🚲 V

Cobalt Cafe & Gallery
(4, D3) €
Café
This gorgeous, elegant café housed in a bright and airy Georgian drawing room is a must, if you're in the 'hood. Almost opposite the James Joyce Cultural Centre, the menu is simple but you'll relish hearty soups by a roaring fire in winter or bouncy fresh sandwiches and salads in the garden on warmer days.
☎ 873 0313 ✉ 16 Great George's St N ☺ 10am-4.30pm Mon-Fri 🚆 all cross-city 🚲 V

Epicurean Food Hall
(4, C5) €
Food Hall
You'll be spoilt for choice in this arcade that has almost every imaginable type of food stall to whet the appetite. The quality however is hit and miss, but good choices include Itsabagel, Taco Taco and Istanbul House.
✉ Liffey St Lower ☺ 9.30am-5.30pm Mon-Sat 🚆 all cross-city 🚊 Jervis 🚲 V

Halo
€ € € €
French/Irish
Befitting its title, food at Halo is simply divine. A cosmopolitan menu of seared salmon sashimi, monkfish with smoked oysters or duck fillet with sweet potato showcase chef Jean-Michel Poulot's versatile talents. The stylish open-plan room with its high ceilings and understated design attracts fashionistas, models and visiting celebs alike.
☎ 878 2999 ✉ Morrison (5, B1; p99), Ormond Quay ☺ 7-10.30pm, noon-3.30pm Sat & Sun 🚆 all cross-city 🚊 Jervis ♿

Halo is simply divine

Vegetarian Options
Dublin has a surprising number of good vegetarian restaurants as well as a considerable number of regular restaurants offering a reasonable selection of things to graze on. The following vegetarian restaurants also have vegan dishes:
Blazing Salads (6, C1; ☎ 671 9552; 42 Drury St; ☺ 9am-5.30pm Mon-Sat; €)
   Excellent salad bar and sandwiches, but no seating.
Cafe Fresh (6, C2; ☎ 671 9669; Powerscourt Centre; ☺ 9am-5pm Mon-Sat; €)
   Hot meals, smoothies, juices, soups and great toasted focaccias.
Cornucopia (p73)
Govinda (6, B2; ☎ 475 0309; 4 Aungier St; ☺ noon-9pm Mon-Sat; €) Run by
   Hare Krishnas, with daily hot meals and salads.
Juice (p73)

Panem (5, A1) €
Café
Pass this tiny café and you'll be lured in by the aroma of fresh *pains au chocolat* (chocolate-filled croissants), savoury focaccias, almond pastries and 100% Arabica Torrisi coffee from Sicily. Mmmm...and you won't find much cheaper in Dublin.
☎ 872 8510 ✉ 21 **Ormond Quay Lower** ☼ 9am-5.30pm Mon-Sat 🚌 all cross-city 🚇 Jervis 🚭 Ⓥ

Soup Dragon (5, A1) €
Soup
Eat in or take away one of twelve tasty home-made soups, including shepherd's pie or spicy vegetable gumbo. Bowls come in three different sizes and prices include fresh bread and a piece of fruit. Kick-start your day with a healthy all-day breakfast selection: fresh smoothies (€3.95), generous bowls of yogurt, fruit and muesli (€4) or poached egg in a bagel (€3.40).
☎ 872 3277 ✉ 168 **Capel St** ☼ 8am-5.30pm Mon-Fri, 11am-5pm Sat 🚭 Ⓥ

Winding Stair (5, C1) €
Café
The Winding Stair is a dusty old bookshop with a café. It's perfect for reading while you eat soups, savoury crepes or *paninis* (deli-style sandwiches). You'll source anything from a shiatsu massage to a bedsit on the stairway noticeboard.
☎ 873 3292 ✉ 40 **Ormond Quay Lower** ☼ 9.30am-6pm Mon-Sat 🚌 all cross-city Ⓥ

TEMPLE BAR

Bad Ass Cafe (5, C2) € €
American
Yes, Sinéad O'Connor worked here as a waiter. But that's not the only reason to visit – cheerful and family-friendly, the café has big, basic pizzas, pastas and burgers. Pulleys on the ceiling whisk orders to the kitchen. Wine and beer available.
☎ 671 2596 ✉ 9-11 **Crown Alley** ☼ noon-10pm 🚌 all cross-city

Bar Italia (4, B5) €
Italian Café
It's small, noisy and you have to queue for a table, but we love the place. Maybe it's the fantastic Palombini coffee, rich chocolate tart, scrummy pastas or deli counter. Probably though it's the buzz of the Italian staff, whizzing between tables in their frantic, friendly way.
☎ 679 5128 ✉ Unit 4, **The Bookend, Essex Quay** ☼ 8am-5pm Mon-Fri, to 6pm Thu & Fri; 9am-6pm Sat 🚌 all cross-city 🚭 Ⓥ

Cafe Gertrude (5, D2) € €
Café
Just around the corner from Temple Bar, this relaxed café offers tempting hot specials such as Cumberland sausage with mustard mash or goat's cheese *galette* (flat flaky pastry) with *tapenade* (rich olive spread), as well as a range of sandwiches and hefty salads.
☎ 677 9043 ✉ 3-4 **Bedford Row** ☼ 8am-11pm, to midnight Fri & Sat 🚌 all cross-city 🚻 🚭

Take advantage of clear skies at Cafe Gertrude

Café Irie (5, C2) €
Café
The dreadlocked waiter who serves you is about the only connection this hippyish little café has with Jamaica. There's a good choice of exotic veggie combinations in sandwich fillings, such as tofu marinated in sweet chilli and satay or goat's cheese and roasted peppers.
☎ 672 5090 ✉ 11 Fownes St Upper ⏱ 9am-8pm Mon-Sat 🚆 all cross-city ♿ Ⓥ

Chameleon (5, C2) € €
Indonesian
Friendly, characterful and draped in exotic fabrics, Chameleon serves up oodles of noodles and Indonesian classics like satay, *gado gado* (veggies with peanut sauce), nasi goreng and *mee goreng* (spicy fried noodles). If you can't decide, try the *rijsttafel* – a selection of several dishes and rice.
☎ 671 0362 ✉ 1 Fownes St Lower, Temple Bar ⏱ 6-11pm Tue-Sat, to 10pm Sun 🚆 all cross-city ♿ Ⓥ

Eden (5, B2) € € €
Modern Irish
Eden is the epitome of Temple Bar chic with its trendy staff, minimalist surroundings, hanging plants and terrace onto Meeting House Sq. But the food is the real star: Eleanor Walsh's cuisine uses organic seasonal produce, lovingly crafted and complemented by a carefully chosen wine list. Summer evenings on the gas-heated terrace see classic films projected onto the nearby Gallery of Photography (p31).
☎ 670 5372 ✉ Meeting House Sq ⏱ noon-3pm & 6-10.30pm, to 11pm Sat & Sun 🚆 all cross-city ♿ Ⓥ

Elephant & Castle (5, C2) € €
American
If it's massive New York–style sandwiches or towering burgers with matchstick chips you're after, this bustling upmarket diner is just the joint. Be prepared to queue though, especially at weekends, when Elephant & Castle heaves with the hassled parents of wandering toddlers, wealthy suburbanites and hungover 20-somethings, all in pursuit of a carb-fest and quiet corner to peruse the paper.
☎ 679 3121 ✉ 18 Temple Bar ⏱ 8am-11.30pm Mon-Fri, 11.30am-11.30pm Sat & Sun 🚆 all cross-city ♿ Ⓥ

Eden and drinking

Gruel (5, B3) € €
Diner
Run by the same people as the excellent Mermaid Café (p71), Gruel offers more sophisticated food than its name suggests. This funky place sells good food that bursts with flavour: sandwiches to die for (slow roast organic meats or vegetables in a bap), zinging salads and risotto, baked fish or their trademark bangers and mash in the evening. The American-style weekend brunch shouldn't be missed.
☎ 670 7119 ✉ 68a Dame St ⏱ 7am-9.30pm Mon-Fri, 10.30am-4pm Sat & Sun 🚆 all cross-city ♿ Ⓥ

Il Baccaro (5, B3) € €
Italian
Tucked away in a wine cellar on Meeting House Sq, this trattoria's rustic Italian cuisine is richly flavoured and authentic. The Irish

---

Kid Friendly
Kids are welcome at most restaurants but some places will only take child diners during the day or early evening. We've indicated the restaurants which are particularly family-friendly with the ♿ symbol. Highchairs, booster seats and child servings are commonly available and many kitchens will cook up something appropriate if asked.

Table for One

Eating alone in Dublin is rarely a problem, and you're unlikely to feel uncomfortable or a nuisance. Some places have a cosy atmosphere that makes you feel right at home, especially as they tend to attract other single diners with their books all day long. Here are a few:

Cornucopia (p73)

Dunne & Crescenzi (p75)

Ely (p77)

Simon's Place (p74)

Winding Stair (p69)

owner imports wines by the barrel from northern Italy – so grab a carafe, order some bruschetta and settle in for some serious eating.

☎ 671 4597 ✉ Diceman's Corner, Meeting House Sq ⏱ 6-11pm Sun-Fri, from noon Sat 🚌 all cross-city ♿ Ⓥ

Mermaid Café
(5, B3) € € €
Modern European
This American-style bistro with natural wood furniture and abstract canvases on its panelled walls caters to a hip gourmand crowd who appreciate inventive ingredient-led, organic food such as monkfish with buttered red chard or braised lamb shank with apricot couscous. The informal atmosphere, pure food and friendly staff make it difficult to get a table without notice.

☎ 670 8236 ✉ 69 Dame St ⏱ 12.30-2.30pm & 6-11pm Mon-Sat, 12.30-3pm & 6-9pm Sun 🚌 all cross-city ♿ Ⓥ

Monty's of Kathmandu
(5, B3) € €
Nepalese
Ethnic food doesn't get much better than this award-winning spot. People keep returning for Nepalese dishes like *gorkhali* (chilli, yogurt and ginger chicken) or *kachela* (raw marinated meat). Shiva beer complements these hearty dishes.

☎ 670 4911 ✉ 28 Eustace St ⏱ 12.30-2.30pm & 6-11.30pm Mon-Sat, 6-11pm Sun 🚌 all cross-city ♿ Ⓥ

Queen of Tarts
(5, A3) €
Café
Queen of Tarts is the mother of all bakery-cafés with its

mouthwatering array of savoury tarts and filled focaccias, fruit crumbles, and sinful pastries. It's small, so get here early for lunch or take out to the quiet garden at the Chester Beatty Library (p14) nearby.

☎ 670 7499 ✉ Cork Hill ⏱ 7.30am-6pm Mon-Fri, from 9am Sat, from 10am Sun 🚌 all cross-city ♿ Ⓥ

Tea Rooms
€ € €
Modern Irish
Bono must have twisted chef Anthony Ely's arm to get HP sauce put on the brunch menu, albeit alongside a classic corned beef *rosti* (Swiss potato pancake). The Tea Rooms' ambitious menu features classic French cuisine – based equally on fish and meat – with an Irish twist. This is *haute cuisine* stripped of pretension, leaving solid, well-prepared seasonal food that is still beautifully presented and a dream to eat.

☎ 407 0813 ✉ Clarence (5, A2; p98), 6-8 Wellington Quay ⏱ 12.30-2.30pm Mon-Fri & Sun, 6.30-10.30pm Mon-Sat, to 9.30pm Sun 🚌 all cross-city ♿ ♿ Ⓥ

Refuel at Gruel; funkier than the name suggests

WEST OF GRAFTON ST

Avoca Café €€
Modern Irish Café
This airy café was one of Dublin's best-kept secrets – it's hidden above Avoca Handweavers (p61) – until discovered by the Ladies Who Lunch. Battle your way to a table past the designer shopping bags, where you'll relish the delicious, rustic delights of organic shepherd's pie, roast lamb with couscous, or sumptuous salads. There's also a secret takeaway salad bar and hot counter in the basement.
☎ 672 6019 ✉ Avoca Handweavers (2, A2), 11-13 Suffolk St 🕙 10am-5pm Mon-Sat, from 10.30am Sun 🚃 all cross-city ♿ Ⓥ

Aya (6, D1) €€€
Sushi Bar
Attached to the swanky shop Brown Thomas (p54), this Japanese restaurant is the city centre's best. There's a revolving sushi bar where you can eat your fill for €25 between 5pm and 9pm (maximum 55 minutes, excluding Thursday and Saturday) or go à la carte from the great menu. Pick up takeaway or specialist products at the Japanese minimart next door.
☎ 677 1544 ✉ 49-52 Clarendon St 🕙 12.30-10pm Mon-Sat, to 11pm Sat; 1-9.30pm Sun 🚃 all cross-city ♿ Ⓥ

Cafe Bardeli (6, C1) €€
Italian
Cafe Bardeli's pizzas, crowned with imaginative toppings such as potato and rosemary or roasted pepper and goats cheese, and with a crispy base, are probably the best you'll find this side of Naples…well, OK, this side of the Liffey. The home-made pasta menu is equally enticing and favourites such as spag bol or fettucine *amatriciana* are also sold by the family-size bowl. Good, fresh food, at prices that won't break the bank in a buzzing atmosphere. What more could you want, hey?
☎ 677 1646 ✉ 12-13 Great George's St S 🕙 noon-midnight 🚃 all cross-city ♿ Ⓥ

Café Mao (6, C2) €€
Asian
There are generally queues of shoppers and families at Café Mao, being a stone's throw from Grafton St. The theme is Chairman Mao and it serves a mad mix of Oriental dishes, from nasi goreng to western Sumatran lamb *rendang* (slow-cooked dry curry). Anything goes, so eat your tempura with a side of garlic naan, and finish with *tarte tatin* (apple tart).
☎ 670 4899 ✉ 2-3 Chatham St 🕙 noon-10pm, to 11pm Mon-Thu, to 11.30pm Fri-Sat 🚃 all cross-city 🚊 St Stephen's Green ♿ to 7pm Ⓥ

Cooke & Magill (6, C2) €€€
Modern European
Adventurous chef Johnny Cooke makes a welcome return to the scene, this time teamed up with one of Dublin's oldest delis. His loyal well-heeled lady and business clientele clamour for pan-fried duck livers, baked hake with artichoke or Johnny's legendary oysters and champagne on the terrace. Eat Mediterranean sandwiches and roulades at the deli counter downstairs.
☎ 679 0536 ✉ 14 William St S 🕙 noon-5.30pm Mon-Sat, 6-11pm Tue-Sat 🚃 all cross-city ♿

It's easy peasy Lemon squeezy to eat too many crepes

Cornucopia (6, D1) €
Vegetarian
Cornucopia has been around for donkey's years and for hearty vegetarian and vegan dishes, it's still the best. Muscle into the cosy country-style kitchen with both suits and sandals for soups, casseroles and salads that will keep you going all day. There's a vegetarian cooked breakfast as an alternative to porridge, muesli and French toast.
☎ 677 7583 ✉ 19 Wicklow St ⏲ 8.30am-8pm Mon-Sat, to 9pm Thu; noon-7pm Sun 🚇 all cross-city ♿ Ⓥ

El Bahia (6, D1) € €
Moroccan
Dark and sultry, the intimate atmosphere at El Bahia, reputedly Ireland's only Moroccan restaurant, is like that of a desert harem. The food is equally exotic with a range of daily *tagines* (stews), couscous and *bastilles* (chicken- or fish-stuffed pastry) to tempt you. The sweet Moroccan coffee brewed with five warming spices is delicious.
☎ 677 0213 ✉ 1st fl, 37 Wicklow St ⏲ 6-10.30pm, to 11pm Thu-Mon 🚇 all cross-city Ⓥ

Good World (6, C1) € €
Chinese
Dim sum is a must here on Sunday afternoon, but arrive early. Choose from the huge selection of bite-sized treats, sip soothing tea and sink back into the buzz of it all. It's open late.
☎ 677 5373 ✉ 18 Great George's St S

⏲ 12.30pm-2.30am, to 6pm Sun 🚇 all cross-city ♿ Ⓥ

Jaipur (6, B2) € €
Indian
The words 'minimalist' and 'Indian restaurant' aren't common bedfellows in these parts but Jaipur is the exception. With massive glass windows and ne'er a patterned wallpaper in sight, this buzzing place serves up delicious Indian specialties such as Kashmiri lamb, *roghan josh* (rich, spicy lamb curry) and Goan seafood curry.
☎ 677 0999 ✉ 43-46 Great George's St S ⏲ 5-11pm 🚇 all cross-city ♿ Ⓥ

Juice (6, B1) € €
Vegetarian
This hip and healthy restaurant may not convert many bona fide carnivores, though they might feel better for its purist Pacific rim–style fare – *nori* (vegetarian sushi rolls), noodles, casseroles, and wraps with an array of smoothies, organic wines or vegan beers to wash it all down. Pancakes with fruit and the sugar-free fruit crumble are a fine way to complete the experience.
☎ 475 7856 ✉ 73-83 Great George's St S ⏲ 11am-11pm Mon-Sat, to 5pm Sun, early bird dinners 5-7pm Mon-Fri 🚇 all cross-city ♿ Ⓥ

La Maison des Gourmets (6, C2) € €
Café
The city's Francophiles amass at this tiny French café over a bakery – and for

good reason. The menu is small but its *tartines* (open sandwiches) with daily toppings like roast aubergine and pesto, salad specials or plates of charcuterie are divine. Dream of Provence with a traditional country breakfast of meats, cheeses and warm crusty bread. You can also make your own Gallic feast from the downstairs deli's selection of cheeses, brioches, cakes, bread and handmade chocolates. A second deli branch, **Le Petit des Gourmets** (☎ 878 1133) is in the Epicurean Food Hall (p68).
☎ 672 7258 ✉ 15 Castle Market ⏲ 9am-6pm Mon-Sat 🚇 all cross-city Ⓥ

Lemon (6, C1) €
Creperie
Lemon doesn't look like much from the street – until you catch a whiff of those crepes. Then it's straight inside where, within minutes, a sweet or savoury crepe or waffle can be yours in breakneck speed. Get it smothered in ice cream, chocolate sauce, coconut or Grand Marnier and enjoy.
☎ 672 9044 ✉ 66 William St S ⏲ 8am-7.30pm Mon-Fri, to 9.30pm Thu; 9am-7.30pm Sat; 10am-6.30pm Sun 🚇 all cross-city ♿ Ⓥ

Leo Burdock's (6, A1) €
Takeaway Café
A long queue snakes down the road at any hour of the day outside this Dublin institution. And there's a reason for it: thick-cut, real

potato chips and crispy fish wrapped in newspaper to go. Sometimes you just have to do it.
☎ 454 0306 ✉ 2 Werburgh St ⏱ noon-midnight 🚌 all cross-city

Market Bar (6, C2)   € €
Tapas
Don't come here to break it off with a lover (or whisper sweet nothings in their ear for that matter) – they won't hear you. This former sausage factory is a big, noisy place, buzzing with atmosphere. Tapas of chicken stew, marinated mackerel or salted squid will set you up for an evening at the bar but as for the *patatas bravas* (potatoes in spicy tomato sauce), dunked in garlicky salsa? Well, you'd sell your spouse for just another bowl.
☎ 613 9094 ✉ 14a Fade St ⏱ noon-9.30pm Mon-Sat, from 4pm Sun 🚌 all cross-city ♿ 🚲 Ⓥ

Nude (5, D3)   €
Café
Modernist Nude may not be the rarity it once was, with juice bars a-go-go in the city but it still has its own unique identity. Owned by Bono's brother, it takes the fast-food experience to a delicious and healthy extreme with hot Asian wraps, bean casseroles and *spirulina*-spiked juices to go or have on the (plastic-free) spot.
☎ 677 4804 ✉ 21 Suffolk St ⏱ 8am-9pm Mon-Sat, to 9.30pm Thu; 8am-7pm Sun 🚌 all cross-city 🚲 Ⓥ

You'll have to shout your sweet nothings at Market Bar

Odessa (6, C1)   € € €
Mediterranean
Join the city's hipsters for home-made burgers, steaks or daily fish specials in Odessa's loungy atmosphere complete with comfy sofas and retro standard lamps. You might not escape the sofa after a few of Odessa's renowned cocktails, quaffed to a game of backgammon. Weekend brunch is extremely popular: you were warned.
☎ 670 7634 ✉ 13-14 Dame Ct ⏱ 6-11pm, 11.30am-4.30pm Sat & Sun 🚌 all cross-city 🚲 Ⓥ

Shanahan's on the Green (6, C3)   € € € €
American Steakhouse
Dublin's first fine-dining steakhouse is set over three floors of a beautiful Georgian town house. Its 'Oval Office' bar contains memorabilia from US

presidents. The menu has lamb, pork, chicken and seafood, but pride of place goes to beefsteaks, which can set you back around €35 (they're worth every cent).
☎ 407 0939 ✉ 119 St Stephen's Green W ⏱ 6-10.30pm, to 11pm Thu-Sat; 12.30-2pm Fri 🚌 all cross-city 🚉 St Stephen's Green

Simon's Place (6, C2)   €
Café
Simon hasn't had to change the menu of doorstep sandwiches and wholesome vegetarian soups since he first opened shop two decades ago and why should he? His grub is as heartening and legendary as he is. It's a great place to mull over a coffee and watch life go by in the old-fashioned arcade.
☎ 679 7821 ✉ George's St Arcade ⏱ 8.30am-6pm Mon-Sat 🚌 all cross-city Ⓥ

Steps of Rome
(6, D3) €
Italian
You can get rustic pizza slices to take away or quickly whipped-up pasta staples in this tiny kerbside café where real Italians meet. It's always packed and you can't book but service is smart so you'll usually get a table after a few minutes' wait.
☎ 670 5630 ✉ Unit 1, Chatham Ct, Chatham St ☷ 10am-midnight ⧉ all cross-city ⧉ St Stephen's Green Ⓥ

Thornton's
(6, D3) € € € €
Modern European
Contrary to popular local belief you won't actually have to remortgage your home for dinner at Thornton's (unless you splash out on a few bottles of 1945 Château Lafitte Rothschild at a healthy €5000 a pop). In fact, the set menus here offer reasonably good value considering what you're getting: a chance to experience the sublime creations of double Michelin–starred chef Kevin Thornton's team, along with impeccable service, and a seat overlooking St Stephen's Green.
☎ 478 7008 ✉ Fitzwilliam Hotel, 128 St Stephen's Green W ☷ 12.30-2pm & 7-10pm Tue-Sat ⧉ all cross-city ⧉ St Stephen's Green ♿

Trocadero
(6, C1) € € €
Traditional Irish
Seedy burlesque venue from the street and flamboyant *belle époque* bar inside, the Troc is a favourite of thespians, media types and the odd drag queen and Robert Doggett is one of the most charming maîtres d in town. Dinners, served in large portions, are supremely unfashionable but that somehow adds to the charm. The pre-theatre menu is popular, but stick around late to see the real action.
☎ 677 5545 ✉ 3 St Andrew's St ☷ 5pm-midnight Mon-Sat ⧉ all cross-city

EAST OF GRAFTON ST

Dunne & Crescenzi
(2, B3) €
Italian Wine Bar
The good folk who brought us wine by the glass, great coffee, antipasto and *panini* in No 14 have opened another buzzing bar that serves pasta, salad and Italian snacks at prices we like.
☎ 675 9892 ✉ 14 & 16 Frederick St S ☷ 8.30am-9.30pm Mon-Sat, to 10.30pm Tue-Sat; noon-6pm Sun ⧉ all cross-city

Gotham Café
(6, D2) € €
Café
A vibrant, youthful place decorated with framed Rolling Stones album covers, Gotham extends its New York theme to its delicious pizzas, which are named after districts in the Big Apple. The Chinatown or Noho are our favourites, or opt for pasta, crostini or Asian salads. And hey, they love kids here.
☎ 679 5266 ✉ 8 Anne St S ☷ noon-midnight, noon-10.30pm Sun ⧉ all cross-city ⧉ St Stephen's Green ♿ Ⓥ

Business Dining
If you need somewhere suitable to charge up your expense account, the following places offer excellent food, service and atmosphere:
Cooke & Magill (p72)
L'Ecrivain (p77)
Restaurant Patrick Guilbaud (p78)
Roly's Bistro (p79)
Thornton's (above)
Unicorn (p78)

Jacob's Ladder
(2, B3) € € € €
Modern Irish

The stylish restaurant in this 1st-floor drawing room overlooking College Park has long been established as one of the city's best. There's a confidence in Adrian Roche's cooking that ensures the inventive pairing of roast red mullet with crispy noodle cakes and fennel puree, or roast crown of partridge with savoy cabbage work, to simple and delicious effect.
☎ 670 3865 ✉ 4-5 Nassau St ⏱ 12.30-3pm

Frozen with indecision at La Stampa

& 6-10pm Tue-Fri, 12.30-2pm & 6-10.30pm Sat
🚌 all cross-city

La Cave (6, D2) € €
French Wine Bar

From the outside, La Cave looks like it might be an adult bookshop, or a gangster pool hall. Don't be fooled. Wind your way downstairs and you'll discover a chic, Paris-style wine bar with crimson walls, tiny tables and a packed crowd shouting over the Brazilian salsa music. The food is OK, but you're really here for the setting and the superb wine list.
☎ 679 4409 ✉ 28 Anne St S ⏱ 12.30pm-late Mon-Sat, 6pm-late Sun
🚌 all cross-city
🚃 St Stephen's Green
🚶 to 6pm

La Stampa € € €
Modern European

The setting here is both gorgeous and dramatic – the opulent 19th-century La Stampa Hotel (6, D3; p101), draped in richly coloured fabrics and decorated with bright, modern artworks. The food ranges from upmarket fish and chips to organic lamb with Moroccan spices.
☎ 677 8611 ✉ 35 Dawson St ⏱ 6pm-midnight Sun-Thu, to 12.30am Fri & Sat
🚌 all cross-city
🚃 St Stephen's Green

Peploe's (6, E3) € €
Wine Bar

A place like Peploe's reminds you how small Dublin really is. Love or money couldn't get you a table here when it first opened in late 2003 because everyone wanted to experience Barry Canny (formerly of Browne's) new 'creation'. While great-value comfort dishes like smoked haddock fish cake, grills or roast meat and fish keep the mainly business crowd happy, it's the brash, conspiratorial atmosphere in the former bank vault that keeps 'em coming back.
☎ 6763144 ✉ 16 St Stephen's Green N
⏱ noon-11pm
🚌 all cross-city
🚃 St Stephen's Green

AROUND MERRION & FITZWILLIAM SQUARES

Bang Café
(4, E7) € € €
Modern European
One of our favourite restaurants in Dublin, twin restaurateurs Simon and Christian Stokes are onto a winner here. Chef Lorcan Cribbin (head-hunted from London's famous Ivy) whips up a varied but consistently good menu that includes Thai baked sea bass and melt-in-your-mouth roast scallops. Don't leave without trying their heavenly warm chocolate brownie, oozing with chocolate sauce. The atmosphere is young, vibrant and eternally stylish.
☎ 676 0898 ✉ 11 Merrion Row ⏲ 12.30-3pm & 6-10.30pm Mon-Sat, to 11pm Thu-Sat 🚌 10, 11, 13b, 51 ♿

Ely (4, E7)
€ €
Wine Bar
Scrummy home-made burgers, bangers and mash or tasty pasta dishes are some of what you'll find in this basement restaurant. Dishes are prepared with organic and free-range produce from the owner's family farm in Co Clare, so you can rest assured of the quality. There's a large wine list to choose from, with over 70 sold by the glass. The lighting is a bit bright but its friendly, relaxed atmosphere makes it popular with female and lone diners.
☎ 676 8986 ✉ 22 Ely Pl ⏲ noon-3pm Mon-Fri; 1-4pm Sat; 6-9.30pm Mon-Sat, to 10.30pm Thu-Sat 🚌 all cross-city

L'Ecrivain
(4, F8) € € € €
French/Irish
Many foodies consider this the best restaurant in town and the recent acquisition of a star from those guys at Michelin proves they're also in favour of chef Derry Clarke's wonderful creations. Heaven-made combinations of the best local, seasonal produce – wild salmon, Dublin Bay prawns, veal and Barbary duck – are matched with inventive sauces and accompaniments and presented like works of art. An attentive but friendly staff make for a dining experience that is far from stuffy.
☎ 661 1919 🖥 www .lecrivain.com ✉ 112 **Baggot St Lower** ⏲ 12.30-2pm Mon-Fri, 7-10.30pm Mon-Sat 🚌 10, 11, 13b, 51 ♿

Ocean (3, H4)
€ €
Seafood
Popular with local business folk, this is a trendy, minimalist place with big

Late-night Eats
Most kitchens shut around 10pm, but there are some places where you can feed the beast a little later. **Eddie Rocket's** (6, D2; ☎ 679 7340; 7 Anne St S; ⏲ 7.30-1am, to 4.30am Sun-Thu) is a saviour for many a hungry Dub. This cheap and cheerful 1950s-style US diner dishes out anything from breakfast to burgers and fries. Other options are more upmarket, such as **Trocadero** (p75), which jumps till late, and **Juice** (p73), where hip young things suck down organic juices to stave off that inevitable hangover.

windows overlooking the water (and U2's soon-to-be-demolished recording studio). There are plenty of outdoor seats from which to savour oysters, crab cakes or a variety of wraps. ☎ 668 8862 ✉ Charlotte Quay Dock 🕙 noon-11pm Mon-Sat, to 1.30am Sat; 12.30-11pm Sun (kitchen closes 10pm) 🚌 all cross-city 🚴 Ⓥ

Restaurant Patrick Guilbaud
(4, E7) € € € €
French
With two Michelin stars tucked under its belt, this elegant restaurant is one of the country's finest. Service is formal and faultless, chef Guillaume Lebrun's food proudly French and the wine list extensive. Surprisingly, the dishes are not overly fussy; it's just excellent produce, beautifully cooked and decoratively presented. ☎ 676 4192 ✉ 21 Merrion St Upper 🕙 12.30-2.15pm & 7.30-10.15pm Tue-Sat 🚌 all cross-city

Tuck some two Michelin-star food under your belt at Restaurant Patrick Gilbaud

Unicorn
(4, E7) € € €
Italian
Saturday lunch at the Unicorn is a noisy Dublin tradition, as media types, politicos and legal eagles gossip and clink glasses in conspiratorial rapture. At lunch many opt for the antipasto bar, while the bistro-style evening menu features Italian classics, done well and priced to match the fashionable surrounds. ☎ 676 2182 ✉ 12b Merrion Ct, Merrion Row 🕙 12.30-3.30pm & 6-11.30pm Mon-Sat 🚌 10, 11, 13b, 51x

AROUND CAMDEN ST

CYO (4, C8) €
Café
By day you can create your own DIY sandwiches from artisan (or carb-free) breads and a range of delicious fillings, by night munch tapas or a hot special. Cleanse yourself with hand-pressed juices and smoothies, boosted with health-enhancing *guarana*, *spirulina* or ginseng. Dynamic co-owner Paula Mc-Clusker will even work out your weekly detox plan and if you fall from the wagon, there's a deep-fried Mars bar on the menu to cushion your landing. ☎ 4053945 ✉ 22 Wexford St 🕙 7.45am-10pm Mon-Sat, 11am-4pm Sun 🚴 Ⓥ

Liston's (4, C8) €
Café
Lunchtime queues out the door testify that the newly expanded Liston's is undoubtedly the best deli in Dublin. Its sandwiches with fresh, delicious fillings, roasted vegetable quiches, rosemary potato cakes and sublime salads will have you coming back again and again. The only problem is there's too much to choose from. ☎ 405 4779 ✉ 25 Camden St 🕙 8.30am-7.30pm Mon-Thu, to 6.30pm Fri, 10am-6pm Sat 🚌 14, 14a, 15, 83 ♿ 🚴 Ⓥ

BALLSBRIDGE

Bella Cuba
(3, H5) € € €
Cuban
Ignore the fact that the entrance is a little poky, and upstairs you'll find a romantic little place with great daiquiris, salsa music on Friday and Saturday nights, and offbeat dishes like Havana meat pies, black-bean soup, fried yucca fingers and chicken stuffed with chorizo. There's also a host of seafood options.
☎ 660 5539 ✉ 11 Ballsbridge Tce 🕑 noon-3pm Thu & Fri, 5.30-11pm 🚌 5, 7, 7a, 8, 45, 46 🚇 Ⓥ

Expresso Bar
(3, G5) € €
Brasserie
Hidden away on a leafy suburban road off Baggot St, this hip, minimalist place with leather seating and subdued lighting attracts local rock stars and other types normally seen only in the social columns. Top nosh like lamb shank or baked sea bass with lime-and-mint potatoes should keep most folk happy when they're not people-watching over *Hello!* magazine.
☎ 660 0585 ✉ 1 St Mary's Rd 🕑 7.30am-5pm Mon-Fri, to 9pm Tue-Fri; 9am-4.30pm & 6-9pm Sat; 10am-4.30pm Sun 🚌 all cross-city 🚇 Ⓥ

French Paradox
(3, H5) € €
French Wine Bar
This bright and airy wine bar over an excellent wine

shop of the same name serves fine authentic French dishes such as cassoulet, a variety of foie gras, cheese and charcuterie plates and large green salads. All there to complement the main attraction: a dazzling array of fine wines, mostly French, unsurprisingly, sold by the bottle, glass or even 6.25cL taste! A little slice of Paris in Dublin.
☎ 660 4068 ✉ 53 Shelbourne Rd 🕑 noon-3pm & 5-10pm Mon-Sat, noon-4pm Sun 🚌 5, 7, 7a, 8, 45, 46

Roly's Bistro
(3, H5) € € €
Traditional Irish
Roly's is an institution with Dublin's business fraternity – always packed and with reliably good food. There are basics (leek and potato soup) and more adventurous fare (Gorgonzola and asparagus tart) but most people come back for the Kerry lamb, the pork stuffed with rhubarb and apple, or the Irish beef.
☎ 668 2611 ✉ 7 Ballsbridge Tce 🕑 noon-2.45pm & 6-9.45pm 🚌 5, 7, 7a, 8, 45, 46

Rooms with Views
Dublin is not big on views – but the following places have something special to gaze at over lunch:
Eden (p70)
Jacob's Ladder (p76)
Ocean (p77)
Winding Stair (p69)

RANELAGH

Diep Noodle Bar (3, F5) € €
Thai
Relatively new Diep is a funky and welcome addition to Ranelagh's eateries. Top-notch Thai and Vietnamese dishes such as *pad thai* (Thai fried noodles), red snapper vermicelli or seafood rice noodles come to your table at lightning speed. Décor is sparse, modern and clean. It's packed at weekends but you'll get a table early or late without a booking.
☎ 497 6550 ✉ Ranelagh ⏰ 5.30-10.30pm Mon, 12.30-11pm Tue-Fri, 3-11pm Sat & Sun 🚌 11, 11a, 13b 🚃 Ranelagh ♿ 🚶 Ⓥ

Mint (3, F6) € € €
Modern French
The people at Mint are ambitious. Chef Oliver Dunne crossed the water from Gordon Ramsay's Pied à Terre in London and his diverse menu has Michelin Aspirant written all over it, the small room is sleek and low-lit, the service formal but friendly. While the food doesn't always deliver the promise on paper, dishes such as rare peppered tuna *niçoise* show that this new place is well on track in reaching for the stars.
☎ 497 8655 ✉ 47 Ranelagh ⏰ noon-3pm & 6-10pm 🚌 11, 11a, 13b 🚃 Ranelagh ♿

Tribeca (3, G6) € €
American Brasserie
This New York–style brasserie has been packed to the rafters since the day it opened and runs a waiting list fopr tables from 5pm nightly. So what's the big deal? Scrummy dishes such as beef and salmon burgers, rib eye with blue cheese, spicy rare beef salad, and prosciutto and goat's cheese omelettes eaten in a funky interior adorned with photos of yellow cabs, politicians and rabbis.
☎ 4974174 ✉ 65 Ranelagh Rd ⏰ noon-11pm 🚌 11, 11a, 13b 🚃 Ranelagh 🚶 Ⓥ

WORTH THE TRIP

Caviston's € € €
Traditional Seafood
While in Dublin, self-respecting crustacean lovers should make the trip from town out to Caviston's seafood restaurant; it's sure to be a meal to remember. The small, unassuming room is packed for each of the three-daily sittings of local fish and seafood, cooked simply with imaginative ingredients that enhance rather than overpower their flavour. In the deli next door locals buy fresh seafood and gourmet items to whip up at home.
☎ 280 9120 ✉ 59 Glasthule Rd, Sandycove (1, C2) ⏰ sittings noon-1.30pm, 1.30-3pm, 3-5pm Tue-Sat 🚃 Glasthule & Sandycove

Johnnie Fox's € €
Seafood Pub
Ireland's highest pub, Johnnie Fox's is about 45 minutes from the city, in the Wicklow Mountains. Some people find it kitsch and overdone – and the pub sure does go in for a lot of self-promotion – but it's actually an authentic old place full of bric-a-brac, gnarled benches, sawdust floors and crackling open fires. The fabulous seafood dishes and nightly Irish music are two other draws, plus there's the lovely rolling country scenery en route.
☎ 295 5647 ✉ Glencullen (1, C2), Co Wicklow ⏰ food 12.30-9.45pm 🚌 44b from Hawkins St 🚶

Entertainment

Gone are the days when all you could hope for in Dublin was a drink in a grimy pub and a dance at a seedy basement disco. Dublin is now one of Europe's most energetic cities, rejuvenated by wealth, optimism and a predominantly young population out to have a good time.

At weekends, the capital's 700-odd pubs and dozens of clubs are packed to the hilt with locals, as well as tourists on a wild weekend away. Its reputation for fun has made Dublin one of the most popular short-break destinations in Europe, and countless stag and hen parties from the UK arrive every weekend.

Dubliners have a legendary capacity for booze and partying. But if that's not your scene, don't fret – there are plenty of options, from theatre, comedy and film to live music.

Top Spots

The most obvious and popular entertainment area is **Temple Bar**, hen-party central. If gaggles of roaring drunk people are your thing, go for it, if not, you'd better stick with the locals elsewhere.

The area **west of Grafton St** is packed with some great bars and attracts a more discerning crowd. Great George's St S especially is lined with places to drink and dance. **East of Grafton St** are bars, mostly catering to a more upmarket, groomed crowd.

Listings & Bookings

For entertainment listings try the weekly *Hot Press* magazine or free *Event Guide,* available in bars and cafés. The *Irish Times* has a pull-out section (The Ticket) and the *Evening Herald* offers similar, both in Thursday's editions. For listings and a laugh get *The Slate,* a free mag that sticks a pin in Dublin's buoyant ego. Check out www.ticketmaster.ie and www.timeout.com/dublin for electronic listings.

Theatre, comedy and classical concert tickets are usually booked through the venue, while tickets for touring international bands are normally sold through a booking agency. These include **HMV** (6, D2; ☎ 456 9569; Grafton St) and **Ticketmaster** (☎ 1890 925 100).

Feel the rhythm of the night at one of Dublin's many live music venues

Special Events

February *Dublin Film Festival* (www.dubliniff.com) – Various cinemas host big- and small-budget films from Ireland and around the world.

March *St Patrick's Day* (www.stpatricksday.ie) – Held on the 17th, with street parties, green beer, fireworks and a spectacular parade.

March–April *Howth Jazz Festival* – Held on the Easter Bank Holiday in this pretty seaside suburb; most gigs are free.

late May *Mardi Gras* – The last weekend of the month sees in Dublin's gay pride celebration, with a parade and other festivities.

June *Dublin Writers Festival* – Four-day literature festival attracting Irish and international writers to its readings, performances and talks.
Heineken Green Energy Festival (www.heineken.com) – One of the city's prime pop and rock festivals, with local and international bands at various venues.
Women's Mini-Marathon (www.womensminimarathon.ie) – 10km charity run on the second Sunday of the month, attracting up to 35,000 participants.

June–July *Music in the Park* – Free music festival at parks around the city.

August *Dublin Horse Show* (www.rds.ie) – Royal Dublin Society Showgrounds (p95) hosts an international showjumping competition.

September *All-Ireland Finals* – Croke Park (p95) goes wild with the hurling finals (second Sunday of the month) and Gaelic football finals (fourth Sunday).

October *Dublin Theatre Festival* (www.dublintheatrefestival.com) – Two-week festival of theatre, Europe's biggest.
Dublin City Marathon (www.dublincitymarathon.ie) – Last Monday of the month.

November *French Film Festival* – Organised by the French embassy.

December–January *Funderland* (www.funfair.ie) – Two-week traditional funfair at the Royal Dublin Society Showgrounds (p95).

Keep practising, and you might just make the all-Ireland hurling finals at Croke Park

BARS & PUBS

Ireland's licensing laws have been fluctuating like a yo-yo in recent years. An unprecedented extension of pub hours was recently tightened because of public concern about the increase in public order offences on the streets after closing time. Ironically, Ireland still has some of the most conservative drinking legislation in Europe. From Monday to Thursday pubs stop serving at 11.30pm, on Friday and Saturday it's 12.30am, and Sunday 11pm, with half an hour's drink-up time each night. Several city-centre bars have late licences. If no opening hours are given in the listings below, assume the establishment follows normal pub hours.

Modern Bars

Anseo (4, C8) This place might not look much on the outside, or the inside for that matter with its bog-standard carpet and chrome décor, but those underground scenesters Monkey Tennis (who brought us hip dive Thomas House) have worked their magic once more on Friday nights. Anseo now rocks most nights with kicking DJs and a young crowd in the know.
✉ **18 Camden St Lower**
🚌 **16, 83, 123**

Bailey (2, A3) You'd never know it now, but the Bailey has a long history. Once a rebel safe house, Sinn Féin founder Arthur Griffith drank here, as did Michael Collins. Today it's all low lighting and warm minimalist design, attracting a monied crowd for lunch at the outdoor tables.
☎ **670 4939** ✉ **2 Duke St** 🚌 **all cross-city** 🚇 **St Stephen's Green** 🕐 **to 7pm**

Dice Bar (4, A5) Co-owned by singer Huey from the band Fun Lovin' Criminals, the Dice Bar looks like something you'd expect to

find on New York's Lower East Side. Its black and red painted interior, dripping candles and stressed seating, combined with rocking DJs most nights, make it a magnet, attracting Dublin's beautiful beatnik crowds.
☎ **674 6710** ✉ **79 Queen St** 🚌 **25, 37, 39, 79, 90** 🚇 **Smithfield**

Front Lounge (5, A3) The front half of this large, opulent bar is lined with sofas and dark nooks, while the so-called Back Lounge is mood-lit and dressed up with a grand piano and chandelier. It draws a mixed, trendy crowd and is popular with the gay community.
☎ **670 4112** ✉ **33-34 Parliament St** 🚌 **all cross-city** ♿ **good**

Globe (6, C1) One of Dublin's first proper café-bars, the Globe, with its wooden floors and brick walls, is as much a daytime haunt for a good latte as a super-cool watering hole by night. Nightly DJs, a relaxed atmosphere and its friendly, mostly foreign staff keeps the place buzzing with a

mix of hip young locals and clued-in visitors.
☎ **671 1220** ✉ **11 Great George's St S** 🚌 **all cross-city** 🕐 **to 7pm**

Hogan's (6, B2) Once a traditional pub, Hogan's is a large, fashionable bar with red leather couches, mood lighting and an Art-Deco club feel. A popular hang-out for young professionals,

it gets busy at weekends with folks eager to take advantage of the late licence.
☎ 677 5904 ✉ 35 **Great George's St S** 🕐 1-11.30pm Mon-Sat, to 1am Thu, to 2.30am Fri & Sat; 3-11.30pm Sun 🚌 all cross-city 🚶 to 6pm

Market Bar (6, C2) High ceilings, bench seating and the din of a chatty crowd give this huge former sausage factory the atmosphere of Grand Central Station on Christmas Eve. It's fashionable, friendly the food is great and they even bring drinks to your table. Check out the wonderful bar made from dipped-brass bank doors.
☎ 613 9094 ✉ 14a **Fade St** 🚌 all cross-city 🚶 good 🚶

Octagon Bar This swish bar at the Clarence (p98) is owned by U2 and has a domed skylight and lots of wood panelling, but not much character. It attracts a mixed crowd, including the odd celebrity, and can be a

That old black magic; Voodoo Lounge

comfortable place to drink when everything else in Temple Bar is packed.
☎ 670 9000 ✉ **Clarence (5, A2), 6-8 Wellington Quay** 🚌 all cross-city 🚶 good

Ron Blacks (6, D3) Despite its cavernous size, this upmarket watering hole manages to retain an inviting atmosphere, thanks to plenty of warm wooden panelling, leather sofas and huge soft lights. It attracts suity young men and smart-dressed girls who aren't afraid to flash their cash.
☎ 672 8231 ✉ 37 Dawson St 🕐 11am-11.30pm

Mon-Sat, to 2am Thu-Sat; noon-11pm Sun 🚌 10, 14, 14a, 15 🚶 to 7pm

SamSara (6, E3) With its cathedral-like proportions and elaborate Moroccan-style décor, SamSara is an impressive sight. It's best appreciated during the week, as on weekends it becomes a heavily perfumed crush of air-kissing, designer-clad fashionistas (and older, less fashionable men ogling them).
☎ 671 7723 ✉ 36 Dawson St 🕐 noon-midnight Mon-Sat, to 1am Thu, to 2.30am Fri & Sat; noon-11pm Sun 🚌 10, 14, 14a, 15 🚶 to 7pm

Micro-Revolution

A number of microbreweries are challenging the supremacy of Guinness for the hearts and taste buds of Dubliners. The best known is the **Porterhouse Brewing Company** (5, A2; ☎ 679 8847; www.porterhousebrewco.com; 16-18 Parliament St) in Temple Bar, with nine of its own beers as well as an incredible list of international beers and wines.

Another contender is **Messrs Maguire** (5, E1; ☎ 670 5777; 1-2 Burgh Quay), a gigantic 'überbar' spread across three levels that offers five of its own brews, from a creamy porter to the German-style Haus beer.

Last but not least, the **Dublin Brewing Company** (4, A4; ☎ 872 8622; www .dublinbrewing.com; 141-146 King St N; 🕐 9am-5.30pm Mon-Fri) operates during business hours only, selling its four beers, which include the well-loved brew Revolution Red.

Thomas Read's (5, A3)
Folks at this spacious, airy bar, spread across two levels, seem to favour wine and coffee over beer. During the day it's a great place to relax and read the paper. For a more traditional setting its annexe, the Oak, is a great place for a pint.
☎ 670 7220 ✉ 1 Parliament St 🚍 all cross-city 🕏 to 7pm

Village (4, C8) This large venue, spread over two floors, is surprisingly cosy for its size. All wooden cladding, plants and warm lighting, the downstairs free bar packs 'em in for its late licence. Upstairs, the venue puts on medium-sized international and home-grown rock and pop acts most nights.

Going Solo

Dublin is one city where being alone never has to mean being lonely. Some of the most welcoming bars and pubs for solo travellers include:

Globe (p83)
International Bar (p87)
Kehoe's (p87)
Octagon (p84)
Stag's Head (p87)
Thomas Read's (this page)

☎ 475 8555 ✉ 30 Wexford St ⏲ noon-2.30am Mon-Sat, noon-1am Sun 🚍 16, 16a, 19, 19a, 65, 83

Voodoo Lounge (4, A5)
Run by the same crew as Dice Bar (p83), the Voodoo Lounge, on the quays just south of Smithfield, is a long, dark bar with decadent, Gothic Louisiana-style décor. Music is loud and that's the way the young fun-lovin' crowd likes it.
☎ 873 6013 ✉ 37 Arran Quay ⏲ 12.30-11.30pm Mon-Sat, to 2.30am Thu-Sat; 12.30-11pm Sun 🚍 25, 37, 39, 79, 90 🚇 Smithfield

Traditional Pubs

Brazen Head (4, A5)
Reputed to be Dublin's oldest pub, the Brazen Head was founded in 1198, but the present building is a young thing, dating from only 1668. Attracting foreign students and tourists as well as locals, the pub has traditional Irish music on Tuesday, Thursday and Friday, which usually kicks off around 9pm.
☎ 679 5186 ✉ 20 Bridge St Lower 🚍 134 🕏 to 7pm

Doheny & Nesbitt's (4, F8) Opened in 1867 as a grocer's shop, this pub has antique snugs, dark-wood panelling and a pressed-metal roof. It's a favourite

haunt of politicians and journalists, Leinster House (p38) being only a short stroll away.
☎ 676 2945 ✉ 5 Baggot St Lower 🚍 10, 11, 13b, 51x 🕏 to 7pm

Flowing Tide (4, D4)
Directly opposite the Abbey Theatre (p91), the Flowing Tide attracts a great mix of theatregoers, northside locals and the odd thespian downing a quick one between rehearsals. It's loud, full of chat and a great place to drink. What more could you ask for in a pub?
☎ 874 0842 ✉ 9 Abbey St Lower 🚍 all cross-city 🚇 Abbey Street 🕏 to 7pm

Grogan's Castle Lounge (6, C2) Known simply as Grogan's (after the original owner), this old place is a city-centre institution. Long patronised by writers, painters and other bohemian types, it's laid-back and contemplative much of the day. Oddly, drinks are slightly cheaper in the stone-floor bar than in the carpeted lounge.
☎ 677 9320 ✉ 15 William St S 🚍 all cross-city 🕏 to 7pm

Horseshoe Bar A joke in Dublin is that the major political decisions of the day aren't made in parliament but here, in the horseshoe-shaped bar at

Brewing Up a Storm

There's no doubt about it – the pub is the heart of social life in Dublin. It is the place where generation gaps are bridged, social ranks dissolved, inhibitions lowered, tongues loosened, stories told and songs sung.

Many Dublin pubs have a proud history of rebellion, acting as bolt holes for nationalists plotting the overthrow of the British from their bar stools. Other pubs have simply provided a home away from home for generations of workers; a place to chat, drink and forget about life's worries.

Brewing in Ireland probably goes back as far as the Bronze Age, but it was between the 4th and 5th centuries AD that the techniques used for distilling whiskey and brewing beer were perfected by monks who brought the skills back from ecclesiastical jaunts in the Middle East. The first drinks were made as remedies but, by dint of some hard research, the monks soon discovered their intoxicating qualities.

By the 16th century, women in Dublin were brewing and distilling in their homes for family and friends. Those who made a superior brew soon acquired a reputation and began selling their surplus stock to outsiders. Thus, the alehouse and 'the local' were born. The industry boomed, and by the 17th and 18th centuries it was estimated that a third of the city's houses sold ale.

It wasn't long before men cottoned on to the potential for money-making and in the late 18th century professional distillers and brewers came onto the scene. Arthur Guinness was one of the first to emerge (p13), setting up shop on the site of a failed brewery in St James's Gate in 1759 and the rest is history. John Jameson joined the fray in 1780, establishing the Smithfield whiskey distillery (p30) on Bow St in 1792.

Today there are almost 100 brands of Irish whiskey, and most of them you will only find in Ireland, so get tasting. Popular brands include Power's, Paddy and Bushmills. As for beer, home-grown talents to watch out for include: Kilkenny-brewed Smithwick's, Beamish Red Ale from Cork, Caffrey's Irish Ale from Antrim, McCardles Traditional Ale, and the growing number of beers offered by Dublin's burgeoning microbreweries (p84).

Other beers just don't stack up to the fine brews available in Dublin

the Shelbourne Hotel (p99). Politicians of every hue rub shoulders with journalists and businessfolk in a fairly relaxed atmosphere, despite the rather grand surrounds. ☎ 676 6471 ✉ **Shelbourne Hotel (4, E7), St Stephen's Green** 🕙 **10.30am-11pm Mon-Sat** 🚌 **all cross-city** 🚊 **St Stephen's Green** ♿ **good** 🚶 **to 7pm**

International Bar (6, C1) A fantastic old pub adorned with stained glass and mirrors, it's famous for its comedy nights and live jazz and blues sessions on Friday and Saturday. Ardal O'Hanlon, who played Dougal in *Father Ted*, started his career here doing stand-up comedy. ☎ 677 9250 ✉ **23 Wicklow St** € **€10/8** 🕙 **comedy Mon, Wed, Thu & Sat 9pm** 🚌 **all cross-city**

Kehoe's (6, D2) One of Dublin's most atmospheric pubs, with a beautiful Victorian bar, a comfy snug and plenty of other little nooks and crannies. Upstairs, drinks are served in what was once the publican's living room — and it looks it. ☎ 677 8312 ✉ **9 Anne St S** 🚌 **all cross-city** 🚶 **to 7pm**

Long Hall (6, B2) With ornate Victorian woodwork, mirrors and chandeliers, this is one of the city's most beautiful and best-loved pubs. From musk-coloured walls to mirrored columns behind the bar, it's all elegantly dingy. The bartenders are experts at their craft,

an increasingly rare sight in Dublin these days. ☎ 475 1590 ✉ **51 Great George's St S** 🚌 **16, 16a, 19, 19a, 65, 83** 🚶 **to 6pm**

Mulligans (5, F1) Built in the 1850s, Mulligans has changed little since then. A place for serious drinking, it is reputed to serve the best Guinness in Ireland and is popular with journalists from the nearby *Irish Times*. The pub appeared as the local in the film *My Left Foot* with Daniel Day-Lewis. ☎ 677 5582 ✉ **8 Poolbeg St** 🚌 **14, 44, 47, 48, 62** 🚊 **Tara Street** 🚶 **to 5pm**

O'Neill's (5, D3) A labyrinthine old pub near Trinity College, O'Neill's dates from the late 19th century, though a tavern has stood on this site for more than 300 years. The odd combination of students and stockbrokers lends a chaotic air. Good food too. ☎ 679 3671 ✉ **2 Suffolk St** 🚌 **all cross-city** 🚶 **to 6pm**

Palace Bar (5, E2) With its mirrors, etched glass and wooden niches, Palace

Bar is often said to be the perfect example of an old Dublin pub. It's popular with journalists from the nearby *Irish Times* and was patronised by writers Patrick Kavanagh and Flann O'Brien last century. ☎ 677 9290 ✉ **21 Fleet St** 🚌 **all cross-city** 🚶 **to 6pm**

Stag's Head (5, C3) Built in 1770 but remodelled in 1895 at the height of Victorian opulence, this pub has magnificent stained glass, chandeliers and marble, carved wood and, of course, mounted stags' heads. It can get crowded but it's worth it; the food's good too. ☎ 679 3701 ✉ **1 Dame Ct** 🚌 **all cross-city** 🚶 **to 6pm**

Toner's (4, E8) With its stone floor and old grocers shelves and drawers, Toner's feels like a country pub in the heart of the city. Though Victorian, it's not elaborate and draws a mainly business crowd. It's not touristy but many visitors seek out its simple charms. ☎ 676 3090 ✉ **139 Baggot St Lower** 🚌 **10, 11, 13b, 51x** 🚶 **to 7pm**

Traditional Irish Music

Cobblestone (4, A4)
Bordering Smithfield Sq, this great old spit-on-the-floor bar features traditional and folk musicians, who usually play until after closing time. The quality of the music is excellent.
☎ 872 1799 ⊠ 77 King St N € €8-12 🚌 134 🚇 Smithfield

Comhaltas Ceoltóirí
Éireann Serious aficionados of traditional music should make the trip towards Dun Laoghaire. The name (*coltas kyohl-thori* erin) means 'Fraternity of Traditional Musicians of Ireland'. It's here that you'll find the best Irish music and dancing in Dublin, with some of the country's top players. The 'craic is mighty' at Friday night's ceilidh (group Irish dance).
☎ 280 0295 ⊠ 35 Belgrave Sq, Monkstown (1, C1) 🖥 www .comhaltas.com € free-

€3, ceilidh €8 🕑 9pm-midnight Tue, Wed, Fri & Sat 🚌 7, 7a, 8 from Trinity College 🚇 Seapoint

Harcourt Hotel (4, D9)
This is one of Dublin's long-running traditional music venues, with lively sessions from class acts in the residents' bar most Friday to Monday nights.
☎ 478 3677 ⊠ 60-61 Harcourt St 🕑 music 9.30pm-late 🚌 15, 15a, 20, 61, 86 🚇 Harcourt

Hughes' Bar (4, B5)
By day this pub is popular with barristers and their clients from the nearby Four Courts, and the early opening hours cater for the workers from the market across the street. But by night the place transforms into a traditional music venue, where you might also see some line-dancing.
☎ 872 6540 ⊠ 19 Chancery St 🕑 7am-11.30pm

Mon-Sat, to 12.30am Thu-Sat; 7-11pm Sun 🚌 all cross-city 🚇 Four Courts 🚶 to 7pm

O'Donoghue's (4, E7)
O'Donoghue's is the most renowned traditional music bar in Dublin, where well-known folk group the Dubliners started out in the 1960s. On warm summer evenings a young, international crowd spills into the courtyard beside the pub.
☎ 676 2807 ⊠ 15 Merrion Row 🚌 10, 11, 13b, 51x 🚶 to 7pm

Oliver St John Gogarty's
(5, D2) The traditional music sessions at this jumping Temple Bar pub are extremely popular with tourists. Come early to get a seat.
☎ 671 1822 ⊠ 58-59 Fleet St 🕑 sessions 2.30-7pm & 9pm-2am Mon-Sat; noon-2pm, 5-7pm & 8.30pm-1am Sun 🚌 all cross-city 🚶

DANCE CLUBS

Most clubs open just before the pubs close – between 11pm and midnight – and close at 2.30am or 3am. Entry to most is between €6 and €9 on weekdays, and up to €20 at weekends. Clubs transform themselves every night of the week, catering to diverse musical (and sexual) orientations. To find what suits you pick up a listings guide (p81).

Lillies Bordello (2, A3)
The newly revamped Lillies is strictly for Big Hairs, wannabes and visiting rock stars. Don't think you'll get within a hair's breadth of celebs though, as they'll be whisked out of view and into the VIP room in a flash. As you might expect, the music is mostly

safe and commercial.
☎ 679 9204 🖥 www .lilliesbordello.ie ⊠ Adam Ct € €7-15 🕑 11pm-3am 🚌 all cross-city

PoD (4, D9)
PoD ('Place of Dance'), is Dublin's renowned nightclub. A metal-Gothic cathedral of dance,

it attracts a large weekend crowd of twentysomethings for its house, techno and Detroit sounds. To get past the notoriously difficult bouncers you'll really need to look the part.
☎ 478 0166 🖥 www .pod.ie ⊠ 35 Harcourt St € €6-15 🕑 11pm-3am

Thu-Sat 🚌 14, 15, 65, 83 🚇 Harcourt

Renard's (2, B3) Run by Colin Farrell's godfather and his favourite den of iniquity, Renard's was once renowned for its 'lock-ins'. An intimate club, it likes its patrons to dress up and has a strict door policy when busy. Music is mainly house, with soul, funk and jazz making the odd appearance. Celebs hang in the difficult-access upstairs bar. ☎ 677 5876 🖳 www .renards.ie ✉ Frederick St S € free-€5 🕑 10.30pm-2.30am 🚌 all cross-city

Rí Rá (6, C1) One of the city's friendlier clubs, this place is full most nights. Refreshingly, the bouncers here are friendly, funny and very fair. The emphasis is on funk, old and new, with ne'er a house beat to be heard on the downstairs floor. Upstairs the Globe bar converts into a chilled-out drink and chat area. ☎ 677 4835 ✉ Dame Ct € €6-10 🕑 11.30pm-3am Mon-Sat 🚌 all cross-city

Spy (6, C2) In a beautiful Georgian building in the Powerscourt Centre (p54), Spy attracts the fine young things in search of a good time. The easy-access club in the small vaulted basement, Wax, is strictly for dancing and drinking, while upstairs an exclusive door policy ensures that only minor celebrities and the rich and beautiful gain access.

☎ 677 0014 ✉ 59 William St S € free-€8 🕑 upstairs 6pm-2.30am Mon-Thu, 5pm-2.30am Fri & Sat; downstairs 11pm-2.30am Mon & Thu-Sat 🚌 all cross-city

Temple Bar Music Centre (5, B2) TBMC combines a live venue, club, bar and café with rehearsal rooms, music classes and recording studios. It's a bit sparse on comfort but music-wise there's something on nightly to suit every taste, from funk and disco to guitar-driven indie rock. A popular salsa class is held on Tuesday at 7.30pm, with a salsa club following at 10.30pm. ☎ 670 9202 🖳 www .tbmc.ie ✉ Curved St 🕑 7.30m-2.30am 🚌 all cross-city

CINEMAS

Irish Film Institute (IFI) (5, B3) The IFI shows classics and new independent flicks. You have to be a member to see a movie here, but you can buy a one-week membership when you buy your ticket; it's only €1.30 per group of any size. The complex also has a bar, café and excellent bookshop. ☎ 679 5744 🖳 www .fii.ie ✉ 6 Eustace St € matinees €5.10/4.45, evenings €6.50/5.50 🕑 centre 10am-11.30pm, films 2-11pm 🚌 all cross-city 🦽 good

Savoy (4, D4) An old-style four-screen, first-run cinema for general releases with late-night shows at weekends. ☎ 874 6000 ✉ O'Connell St Upper € before 6pm €5.60/4.60, after 6pm €7.50/4.60 🕑 2-11pm 🚌 all cross-city 🚇 Abbey Street 🦽

Screen (5, F1) Between Trinity College and O'Connell Bridge, Screen shows fairly good art-house and indie films on its three screens. ☎ 672 5500 ✉ 2 Townsend St € before 6pm €5.60/4.60, after 6pm €7.50/4.60 🕑 2-10.30pm 🚌 5, 7, 7a, 8, 14 🚇 Tara Street 🦽

UGC Multiplex (4, C4) A massive 17-screen cinema, which replaced many smaller cinemas, showing general and Irish releases. Late shows Friday and Saturday night start around 11.30pm. ☎ 872 8400 ✉ Parnell Centre, Parnell St € €7.50/4.70-5.50 🕑 11.30am-11.30pm, to 1.30am Fri & Sat 🚌 all cross-city 🚇 Jervis 🦽 good

Step out to the IFI

ROCK, JAZZ & BLUES

Ambassador Theatre (4, D3) This former cinema, at the top of O'Connell St, has thankfully kept much of its rococo interior intact. The view of its international acts on stage is better from the spacious downstairs auditorium, while on the mezzanine level it's seating only in old cinema seats complete with drinks holders.
🖳 www.mcd.ie ✉ O'Connell St ⏰ doors open 7.30pm 🚌 all cross-city

Crawdaddy (4, D9) Like a stylish speakeasy with its velvet drapes and dripping candles, you can't help but lie back, bourbon in hand and listen to the tuneful international jazz, folk and acid jazz acts. Opened in May 2004, this small and intimate jazz café is the latest addition to the old Harcourt Street Station complex.
☎ 478 0166 ✉ Harcourt St € €20-35 ⏰ 7.30pm-3am Wed-Sat 🚌 14, 15, 48a 🚈 Harcourt

Electric (4, D9) Also located in the old Harcourt Street Station complex, this newly expanded 3000-capacity place (formerly Red Box) is one of the best venues for dance gigs, with top European dance bands and DJs strutting their stuff to a largely young crowd. Expect queues at weekends.
☎ 478 0166 ✉ Harcourt St € €20-35 ⏰ 7.30pm-3am Wed-Sat 🚌 14, 15, 48a 🚈 Harcourt

The Big Gigs

Big international acts increasingly include Dublin on their tour circuits. Here's where they usually play:

Croke Park (4, E1; ☎ 855 8176; www.crokepark.ie; Clonliffe Rd) 65,000-capacity GAA stadium that hosts the odd concert.

Lansdowne Rd Stadium (3, H4; ☎ 668 9300; Ballsbridge, Dublin 4) Normally a rugby and football ground, it's also used for the occasional rock concert.

Point Depot (3, H3; ☎ 836 3633; www.thepoint.ie; East Link Bridge, North Wall Quay) Originally a rail terminus and quite soulless, but with a capacity of 6000.

Royal Dublin Society Showgrounds (3, H5; ☎ 668 0866; www.rds.ie; Ballsbridge, Dublin 4) Open-air show-jumping arena that holds 40,000.

Slane Castle (☎ 041-982 4207; www.slanecastle.ie; Slane, County Meath) 46km northwest of Dublin, home to the annual August Slane Festival and the odd special gig, like a U2 concert.

One of the less popular events at Croke Park Stadium

JJ Smyth's (6, B3) Jazz and blues nightly at this friendly pub draws a regular crowd of dedicated music lovers. The Irish Blues Club plays on Tuesday, and long-standing resident bands from Thursday to Monday.
☎ 475 2565 ✉ 12 Aungier St € €5-8 🕙 most shows start 8.30-9.30pm 🚌 16, 16a, 19, 19a, 65, 83

Vicar St (4, A6) Smaller rock, folk and jazz performances take place at this venue near Christ Church Cathedral. Though it seats 1000 between its table-serviced area and theatre-style balcony, it retains an intimate atmosphere with low lighting and an excellent sound system. Neil Young, Bob Dylan and Justin Timberlake have all played here.
☎ 454 5533 🖳 www .vicarstreet.com ✉ 58-59 Thomas St 🚌 51b, 78a, 123, 206

Whelan's (4, C8) A good gig here can be quite magical. The crowd gathers round the elevated central stage and more peer down from the circular balcony – everyone mouthing the words to their favourite songs and ballads. Whelan's has an interesting parade of fine local and international singer-songwriters – well worth a look.
☎ 478 0766 🖳 www .whelanslive.com ✉ 26 Wexford St (enter via Camden Row) € €8-16 🕙 doors open 8pm 🚌 14, 15, 65, 83

THEATRE & COMEDY

Theatre bookings can usually be made by quoting a credit-card number over the phone; you can collect your tickets just before the performance. Most plays begin between 8pm and 8.30pm.

Abbey Theatre (4, E4) Together with the more experimental Peacock Theatre on the same premises, the Abbey is Ireland's national theatre. The theatre shows work by established contemporary Irish writers as well as classics by WB Yeats, JM Synge, Sean O'Casey and Samuel Beckett. At the Peacock works tend to be by young writers and performed by less-established actors.
☎ 878 7222 🖳 www .abbeytheatre.ie ✉ Abbey St Lower € Abbey €12-25, Peacock €10-15 🕙 box office 10.30am-7pm Mon-Sat 🚌 all cross-city 🚉 Abbey Street ♿ good 🚻

Andrew's Lane Theatre (5, C3) A well-established, commercial fringe theatre that shows work by touring local companies and overseas productions, often comedy or light drama.
☎ 679 5720 🖳 www .andrewslane.com ✉ 9-17 St Andrew's Lane € free-€18 🕙 box office 10.30am-7pm Mon-Sat 🚌 all cross-city ♿ good 🚻

Crypt Arts Centre An atmospheric and intimate space housed in the crypt of the Chapel Royal (6, B1), this venue serves many of Dublin's young, up-and-coming companies, as well as the odd live music performance. Tragedies and philosophical works are often attempted.
☎ 671 3387 🖳 www .cryptartscentre.org ✉ Dublin Castle, Dame St € €10-12/7.50 🕙 box office 1-5pm Mon-Fri, 10am-6pm Sat 🚌 all cross-city

Gaiety Theatre (6, C3) Opened in 1871, this Victorian theatre was restored to its former glory several years ago. Its repertoire is diverse, from modern plays, musicals, comedies and revues to Shakespeare. Opera Ireland have a season here and on Friday and Saturday nights the venue is taken over by salsa and soul clubs until 4am.
☎ 677 1717 🖳 www .gaietytheatre.net ✉ King St S 🕙 box office 10am-7pm Mon-Sat 🚌 all cross-city 🚉 St Stephen's Green 🚻

Gate Theatre (4, D3) International classics from the likes of Harold Pinter and Noel Coward, older Irish works by playwrights such as Oscar Wilde, George Bernard Shaw and Oliver Goldsmith, as well as newer

Behan there, done that

Novelist, playwright and journalist Brendan Behan was a legendary Dublin hell-raiser and drinker whose antics regularly landed him in prison and hospital, and had him barred from dozens of pubs. In his short but eventful life he did time for IRA activities and the attempted murder of a policeman, was a columnist for the *Irish Press*, and then turned to literature. His books include *Borstal Boy* and *The Scarperer* and a celebrated play *The Hostage*. Sadly, his lifestyle got the better of him and he died of cirrhosis of the liver in 1964, aged 40.

plays are performed here. ☎ 874 4045 🖥 www .gate-theatre.ie ✉ Parnell Sq € €15-25 🕐 box office 10am-7pm Mon-Sat 🚍 all cross-city

Ha'penny Bridge Inn (5, C2) From Tuesday to Thursday you can hear some pretty funny comedians (and some truly awful ones) do their shtick in the upstairs room of this Temple Bar pub. Tuesday night's Battle of the Axe, an improv night that features a lot of crowd participation, is the best.
☎ 677 0616 ✉ 42 Wellington Quay € €8/6 🕐 shows start 9pm Tue-Thu 🚍 all cross-city

Hub (5, B3) Friday night's Leviathan cabaret club features wise-cracking political satire from a range of home-grown and visiting stand-ups and commentators, hosted by rising TV comic Dara O'Briain.
☎ 635 9991 ✉ Eustace St € €15 🕐 8pm-late 🚍 all cross-city

Laughter Lounge (4, D5) Dublin's only purpose-built comedy venue reopened in October 2004 after a major overhaul. It can squeeze in 400 punters for live

Crowds flocking to see the Olympia Theatre's latest show

shows, which feature four high-quality Irish and international acts each night.
☎ 1800 266 339 ✉ Eden Quay € €20 🕐 shows start 9pm Thu-Sat 🚍 all cross-city 🚇 Abbey Street ♿ good

Olympia Theatre (5, B3) This is an ornate old Victorian music hall that specialises in light plays, comedy and, at Christmas time, panto. In recent years though, this pleasantly tatty place has gained more of a reputation for its live gigs, including performances by some big international acts.

☎ 677 7744 ✉ 72 Dame St 🕐 box office 10am-6.30pm Mon-Sat 🚍 all cross-city ♿

Project Arts Centre (5, B2) The newly renovated Project Arts Centre's three stages (including a black box) are home to experimental plays from up-and-coming Irish and foreign writers. Some are brilliant, others execrable, but there's excitement in taking risks.
☎ 1850 260027 🖥 www .project.ie ✉ 39 Essex St E 🕐 box office 11am-7pm Mon-Sat 🚍 all cross-city ♿ good ♿

CLASSICAL MUSIC & OPERA

Classical music in Dublin has had a hard time of it, plagued by inadequate funding and questionable repertoires. Things are improving, though, and the scene is regularly enhanced by visiting performers and orchestras.

Bank of Ireland Arts Centre (5, D2) Apart from art exhibitions and the banking museum, the arts centre hosts free lunchtime recitals every two weeks or so, as well as an evening programme of concerts. ☎ 671 1488 ⌨ www.bankofireland.ie ✉ Foster Pl ☽ box office 11am-4pm Tues-Fri 🚌 all cross-city

National Concert Hall (4, D8) Ireland's premier classical concert venue, the National Concert Hall, hosts performances by the National Symphony Orchestra and international artists. There's also jazz, traditional Irish and other contemporary concerts. From June to September it puts on inexpensive concerts on Tuesdays from 1.05pm to 2pm. ☎ bookings 417 0000, info 417 0077 ⌨ www.nch.ie ✉ Earlsfort Tce ☽ box office 10am-7pm Mon-Sat 🚌 10, 11, 13, 14, 15, 44, 86 🚇 Harcourt ♿ good ☀ special summer concerts

RDS Concert Hall The huge concert hall at the Royal Dublin Society Showgrounds (3, H5) hosts a rich and varied programme of classical music and opera throughout the year, featuring both Irish and international performers. ☎ 668 0866 ✉ Ballsbridge ⌨ www.rds.ie 🚌 5, 7, 7a, 8, 45 🚇 Sandymount ♿ good ☀

You can bank on seeing good concerts at the Bank of Ireland

Music of the Gods

Many of Dublin's churches have accomplished choirs that make full use of the heavenly acoustics, including:

Christ Church Cathedral (p15) Come to hear choral evensong four times a week (call for more information).

St Ann's Church (6, E2; ☎ 676 7727; Dawson St; 🚌 10, 11, 13b, 14, 14a, 20b) Free lunchtime organ recitals in July and August on Thursdays at 1.15pm (call for details).

St Patrick's Cathedral (p23) Hear the choir sing evensong and try to book tickets for the carols performed around Christmas

St Stephen's Church (p33) The acoustics in the 'Peppercanister Church' are superb and it hosts concerts on an ad hoc basis.

GAY & LESBIAN DUBLIN

The fabulous Mardi Gras takes place over the last weekend in May, while the annual Alternative Miss Ireland pageant usually runs during the third weekend in March. For details of both festivals call ☎ 873 4932.

Boilerhouse Sauna (5, A3) This is a popular late-night destination for people looking to sweat it out after partying at George (below), just around the corner. It's big and very clean and is reputed to be the best-run of Dublin's saunas.
☎ 677 3130 ⊠ 12 Crane Lane € €15 ⏰ 1pm-4am Sun-Thu, 24hr Fri & Sat 🚌 all cross-city

George (6, B1) You can't miss the bright-purple George, Temple Bar's only overtly gay bar, which has a reputation for becoming ever more wild and wacky as the night progresses. At 6.30pm on Sunday it is packed for an enormously popular bingo night, while Thursday night is the Missing Link game show hosted by Annie Balls.
☎ 478 2983 ⊠ 89 Great George's St S € most nights €5-8 after 10pm ⏰ 12.30-11.30pm Mon & Tue, 11.30pm-2.30am Wed-Sat, 12.30pm-1am Sun 🚌 all cross-city

Gubu (5, A1) Run by the owners of Globe (p83) and Front Lounge (p83), 'Gaybu' is a stylish bar with stressed metal and chunky furniture. Wednesday's comedy night with Busty Lycra, is popular.
☎ 874 0710 ⊠ Capel St ⏰ 4-11.30pm, to 12.30am Thu-Sat 🚌 37, 70, 134, 172 🚇 Jervis

Out on the Liffey (4, B5) The northside's gay and lesbian stronghold for many years, this pub has developed a bit of a rough reputation, mostly due to party drugs. It still a great bar, despite the presence of ever-watchful bouncers. Sunday is the popular karaoke night, open to both men and women.
☎ 872 2480 ⊠ 27 Ormond Quay Upper ⏰ 11am-11pm, to 11.30pm Mon-Sat 🚌 all cross-city

Bingo with transvestite Miss Shirley Temple-Bar at George

Gay Club Nights

Plenty of clubs in Dublin run gay and lesbian nights. Though the scene is constantly changing, the following nights have built up a steady following in recent times:

HAM Friday night at PoD (p88) is 'Homo Action Movies', one of Dublin's most enduring gay nights, with uplifting and progressive House. Every second week the 'Gristle Cabaret' precedes 'HAM'.

Kiss is the latest popular all-girls night at Vicar St (p91) held on the third Sunday and last Friday of the month. Music is chart-driven, including slow sets, but the crowd is surprisingly eclectic.

Strictly Handbag Monday-night club at Rí Rá (p89) attracts a mixed, but heavily gay, crowd for cheesy and sleazy '80s hits downstairs and '60s and '70s pop upstairs. Pre-club knees-up at the Front Lounge (p83) from 9pm.

SPORTS

Football

Along with hurling, **Gaelic football** is Ireland's major **Gaelic Athletics Association** (www.gaa.ie) sport. Like hurling, it's a high-speed, aggressive game, but uses a round ball that is kicked along the ground soccer-style, or passed between players as in rugby. It's not dissimilar to Australian Rules football and some Gaelic stars have gone on to make it big in Oz. The All Ireland final takes place in September, at Croke Park (below).

While hurling and Gaelic football have their greatest following in rural Ireland, **football** (soccer) and **rugby** (www.irishrugby.ie) are probably more popular in Dublin. Support for British soccer teams, especially Manchester United, Liverpool and Glasgow Celtic, is high, though the Irish national team also attracts a full house when it plays. For details of international matches contact the **Football Association of Ireland** (☎ 676 6864; www.fai.ie). Ireland is also a power in world rugby and great attention is paid to the annual **Six Nations Championship**

Major Sporting Venues

Croke Park (4, E1; ☎ 836 3222; www.crokepark.ie; Dublin 3; 🚌 3, 11, 11a, 16, 16a, 51a from O'Connell St (4, D4); 🚆 Connolly Station)

Fairyhouse Racecourse (1, B1; ☎ 825 6167; www.fairyhouseracecourse.ie)

Harold's Cross Park (3, E6; ☎ 497 1081; 151 Harold's Cross Rd; 🚌 16, 16a, 19a, 49)

K Club (1, B1; ☎ 601 7200; www.kclub.ie; Straffan, Co Kildare)

Lansdowne Rd Stadium (3, H4; ☎ 668 4601; Ballsbridge; 🚆 Lansdowne Rd)

Leopardstown (1, C2; ☎ 289 3607; www.leopardstown.com; Foxrock, Dublin 18; 🚌 from Eden Quay (4, E4) on race days)

Royal Dublin Society Showgrounds (3, H5; ☎ 668 0866; www.rds.ie; Ballsbridge; 🚌 5, 7, 7a, 8, 45; 🚆 Sandymount)

Shelbourne Greyhound Stadium (3, H4; ☎ 668 3502; Ringsend; 🚌 3 from O'Connell St (4, D4))

They've got the team, the net and some uniforms; all they need now is the ball...

(www.6nations.net), which pits Ireland against England, Wales, Scotland, France and Italy. Even more passion is likely to be roused when the national team plays Australia. International soccer and rugby matches take place at Lansdowne Rd Stadium (p95) in Ballsbridge.

Golf

The popularity of Ireland's fastest-growing sport, **golf** (www.golf.ireland.ie), is due in part to the success of Irish golfers such as Darren Clarke, Padraig Harrington and Paul McGinley. The Smurfit European Open takes place in late July/early August at the **K Club** (p95) in Co Kildare, which was designed by Arnold Palmer.

Hurling

For the uninitiated, hurling is a fascinating game to watch. It combines elements of hockey and lacrosse – players hit the ball along the ground or through the air or even carry it on the end of their hurley or caman. Fast-paced and furious, the skills displayed are astounding. Dublin isn't a great power in the world of hurling – the best teams come from Kilkenny and Cork. The All Ireland Hurling Final at Croke Park (p95) takes place in September attracting crowds of more than 80,000.

Racing

The Irish just love **horse racing** (www.hri.ie), a fact that can be easily witnessed at racetracks on the outskirts of Dublin. Leopardstown (p95) in southern Dublin is the home of the prestigious Hennessey Gold Cup, which runs in February. The Irish Grand National is held on Easter Monday at Fairyhouse (p95), which you'll find 9km northwest of Dublin in County Meath.

Greyhound racing takes place at Harold's Cross Park (p95), just a short hop from the city centre, and at the more comfortable Shelbourne Greyhound Stadium (p95) in Ringsend, which is only 10 minutes away from the centre. Races are usually held two or three times a week from February through to early December; call to check days and starting times (they usually begin around 7.30pm).

Still life with hurling stick and ball

Sleeping

Dublin is one of Europe's more expensive cities to sleep in, and until you reach the upper price brackets, you're not always getting great value for money. Dublin's tourism boom also means that in high season – from around May to September – getting the room you want, at a reasonable price, can be a challenge. New hotels are opening all the time but it's still wise to book well ahead.

If you're only in Dublin for the weekend, you'll want to stay in the city centre or a short stroll away. Not surprisingly, accommodation south of the Liffey is pricier than that on the northside. While some good deals can be found in the north, most bargains are in less than salubrious areas, where drugs and crime are a problem. If you stay there, keep a close watch on your bags and wallets and take care when walking at night.

Room Rates

The categories used in this chapter indicate the cost per night of a standard double room in high season.

Deluxe	€250–400
Top End	€150–249
Mid-Range	€80–149
Budget	under €79

Most budget to mid-range places charge low and high season rates, and prices are bumped up during holidays, festivals or sporting events. At top-end hotels, always check what discounts are available on the published rack rates by phoning or checking their website. Top-end and deluxe hotels fall into two categories – period Georgian elegance and cool, minimalist chic. No matter what the décor, you can expect luxurious surrounds, king-size beds, satellite TV, in-room videos, full room service, PC/fax connections and discreet, professional pampering.

Dublin's mid-range accommodation is more of a mixed bag, ranging from no-nonsense but soulless chains to small B&Bs in old Georgian town houses. The pricier B&Bs in this category are beautifully decked out and extremely comfortable, while at the lower end rooms are simple, a little worn and often rather overbearingly decorated. Here you can look forward to kitsch knick-knacks, chintzy curtains, lace doilies and clashing floral fabrics so loud they'll burn your retinas. As for breakfast, it can range from home-baked breads, fruit and farmhouse cheeses to a traditional, fat-laden fry-up.

Cheaper B&Bs and hostels make up the budget end, and while they can sometimes be grim, the ones listed here are clean, bright and good value.

Bookings

If you arrive without accommodation, staff at Dublin Tourism's walk-in booking offices will find you a room for €4 plus a 10% deposit.

If you want to book a hotel from elsewhere in Ireland or abroad, the easiest way is to go through Gulliver Info Res, Dublin Tourism's computerised reservations service, via their website www.visitdublin.com. See p120 for a list of Dublin Tourism offices and Gulliver contact numbers.

DELUXE

Clarence (5, A2) Its 1930s penthouse suite, with unrivalled views of the city from its rooftop hot tub, is almost continuously booked out by visiting celebs and rock star friends of hotel owners Bono and the Edge from U2. For the rest of us, the 50-odd lavish rooms, decorated in an ecclesiastical theme with white and cardinal colour schemes, offer the elegant comfort of Egyptian cotton linen, beautifully simple bathrooms, white American oak furniture and original artwork by bandmate, Guggi. A night's kip doesn't come cheap here but you'll rest well, knowing you're in one of the hottest beds in town.
☎ 407 0800 ▢ www .theclarence.ie ✉ 6-8 Wellington Quay ▢ all cross-city Ⓟ ♿ ✗ Tea Rooms (p71) ♿

Four Seasons (3, H5) Some may find the service a little OTT in this branch of the Canadian luxury chain, but probably not the visiting rock stars and dignitaries who are well used to excessive pampering. Though there's something surreal about the mock-antique décor, the rooms are extremely comfortable with DVD players, stereo and minibars to enhance the experience. For just under €122,500 you can share the bed in the presidential suite used by Justin Timberlake, complete with kitchen, two bathrooms and walk-in closet the size of an average Dublin bedsit.
☎ 665 4000 ▢ www .fourseasons.com ✉ Simmonscourt Rd, Ballsbridge ▢ 5, 7, 8, 45, 46 Ⓟ ♿ ✗ Seasons ♿

Gresham (4, D3) Gresham Hotel, a landmark hotel and one of Dublin's oldest and until now, most traditional, underwent a significant facelift in 2002 shedding its cosy granny's parlour look to reveal a brighter, smarter, more modern one. The hotel's apparent clientele – elderly groups on shopping breaks to the capital and well-heeled Americans – has remained loyal. Rooms are spacious and well serviced, though the décor is a little fussy.
☎ 874 6881 ▢ www .gresham-hotels.com ✉ 20-22 O'Connell St Upper ▢ all cross-city ♿ ✗ Aberdeen Restaurant, Toddy's Bar ♿

Merrion (4, E7) This resplendent five-star hotel, in a terrace of beautifully restored Georgian town

View from Clarence's rooftop; unless you're famous, this could be the only time you see it

houses, opened in 1988 but looks like it's been around a lot longer. Try to get a room in the old house (with the largest private art collection in the city), rather than the newer wing, to sample its sophisticated comforts. Its location opposite government buildings and just off Merrion Sq – a predominantly business area – makes for an unusually tranquil weekend setting so close to the city centre.
☎ 603 0600 ▢ www .merrionhotel.com
✉ **Merrion St Upper**
🚌 5, 7, 8, 10, 11, 45
🅿 ♿ ✕ **Restaurant Patrick Guilbaud (p78)** 🐎

Morrison (5, B1) Since opening its doors in 1999, the eternally-hip Morrison has been vying with the Clarence (p98) across the river in the style stakes, for Dublin's coveted title Trendiest Hotel in Town. Hong Kong–Irish fashion designer John Rocha helped create the Morrison's sophisticated-earthy look using his signature velvet throws, dark wood and contemporary white

The Shelbourne Hotel, good for your constitution

furnishings. The loosely Oriental-style rooms are bright, if a little compact, and feature Egyptian cotton linen, CD players, modem facilities and pieces of Rocha's own line of crystal.
☎ 887 2400 ▢ www .morrisonhotel.ie
✉ **Ormond Quay Lower**
🚌 all cross-city 🚊 Jervis ♿ ✕ **Halo (p68)** 🐎

Shelbourne Hotel (4, E7) Founded in 1824, the famous Shelbourne Hotel remains Dublin's grand dame and retains its enduring old-world grandeur. Rooms are spacious and very comfortable with

every modern facility. The Irish Constitution was first drafted here in 1922 and to this day, politicians and hacks can be spotted swigging malt in its Horseshoe Bar. For the more salubrious, the leisure centre and swimming pool provide a healthy alternative. Afternoon cream teas in the drawing room, overlooking St Stephen's Green (p18), are a Dublin institution.
☎ 676 6471 ▢ www .shelbourne.ie ✉ 27 St Stephen's Green 🚌 all cross-city 🚊 St Stephen's Green 🅿 ♿ ✕ **No 27, Side Door** 🐎

TOP END

Harrington Hall (4, D8) This award-winning Georgian guest house, run by the King family, is more like a small private hotel. Extra frills include room and porter service, food and bar menu and data ports in all rooms. Some of the bedroom furnishings are a tad loud but rooms are spacious, impeccably neat and the Georgian features gorgeous.

☎ 475 3497 ▢ www .harringtonhall.com
✉ **70 Harcourt St** 🚌 15, 16, 19 🚊 **Harcourt**
🅿 ♿ ✕ 🐎

Paramount Hotel (5, A3) This boutique-inspired small hotel with more than a nod to the Art Deco era has 70 surprisingly tasteful bedrooms with leather furnishings and stylish

bathrooms. Opt for 2nd-floor bedrooms or higher, unless you want to sing along to tracks from the nightclub below. Considerable reductions are often offered on the website and in low season.
☎ 417 9900 ▢ www .paramounthotel.ie
✉ **Parliament St & Essex Gate** 🚌 all cross-city ♿ ✕ **Turk's Head** 🐎

MID-RANGE

Albany House (4, D8)

You'll forgive this city-centre gem for being a little dog-eared in places because it feels like a genuine Georgian Dublin home. With original features and incredible plasterwork intact, Albany House is spread over three houses. Opt for bright, tastefully furnished modern rooms or bigger original rooms complete with antique furniture. Excellent value.
☎ 475 1092 🖥 www.byrne-hotels-ireland ✉ 84 Harcourt St 🚌 15, 16, 19 🚊 Harcourt ℗ ✖ ♿

Castle Hotel (4, C2)

Established in 1809, the Castle Hotel claims to be Dublin's oldest and has been in the hands of only three families since. Furnishings are likewise traditional and a tad antiquated throughout its 50 rooms, many of which are huge, and with lovely Georgian features intact. There's a fabulous *palazzo*-style grand staircase and the house, though a bit rough around the edges, still feels like an authentic

The Castle Hotel's décor was modern in 1809

19th-century home.
☎ 874 6949 ✉ Great Denmark St 🚌 all cross-city ℗ ✖ Cobalt Cafe & Gallery (p68) ♿

Clifden Guesthouse (4, D2)

This really is a great place to stay in the area. A very nicely refurbished Georgian house with 14 fine, tastefully decorated rooms. They're all en suite, impeccably neat and extremely comfortable.
☎ 874 6364 🖥 www.clifdenhouse.com ✉ 32 Gardiner Pl 🚌 11, 16, 41 ℗ ✖ ♿

Grafton Guesthouse (6, B2)

Under new management of those hip folks down at the Globe (p83) bar, the 17 en suite rooms in this heritage building have been whipped into bright and funky shape. Expect contemporary fittings, stylish walnut furniture, retro wallpaper

Home Away From Home

Self-catering apartments are a good option for visitors staying a few days, for groups of friends, or families with kids. Apartments range from one-room studios to two-bed flats with lounge areas, and include bathrooms and kitchenettes. Good, central places include:

Clarion Stephen's Hall (4, E8; ☎ 638 1111; www.premgroup.com; 14-17 Leeson St Lower) Deluxe studios and suites, with in-room safe, fax, modem facilities and CD players.

Latchfords (4, F8; ☎ 676 0784; www.latchfords.ie; 99-100 Baggot St Lower) Studios and two-bedroom flats in a Georgian town house.

Litton Lane Apartments (4, D5; ☎ 872 8389; www.irish-hostel.com; Litton Lane) Basic and modern two-bedroom flats in a secure riverside complex.

Oliver St John Gogarty's Penthouse Apartments (☎ 671 1822; www.gogartys.ie; 18-21 Anglesea St) Perched high atop the pub (5, D2; p88), these one- to three-bedroom places have views of Temple Bar.

Travelling with Children

Finding reasonable accommodation for a young family can be difficult in Dublin. Your best bet is a larger chain hotel, where a flat room rate usually applies, a serviced apartment, or a hostel where you can house the whole family in one room, usually with en suite. Almost all deluxe and top-end hotels offer 24-hour babysitting services and extra beds or cots. Be warned though that some B&Bs tend to discourage young guests. We have denoted places that are particularly child-friendly with a 👶 .

and all mod must-haves like TVs, data ports and veggie breakfasts at a fine price. ☎ 679 2041 ✉ 26-27 Great George's St S 🖥 all cross-city 👶 ✕ Odessa (p74)

Irish Landmark Trust (5, B3) This fabulous heritage 18th-century house has been gloriously restored to the highest standard by the Irish Landmark Trust charity. You can have this unique house, which sleeps up to seven in its double, twin and triple bedrooms, all to yourself for one or any number of nights. Furnished with tasteful antiques, authentic furniture and fittings (including a grand piano in the drawing room), this kind of period rental accommodation is rare and something really special. ☎ 670 4733 🖥 www .irishlandmark.com ✉ 25 Eustace St 🖥 all cross-city ✕ 👶

Jurys Inn Christchurch (4, B6) This large limited-service hotel directly opposite Christ Church Cathedral (p15) has 182 'cookie-cutter' rooms – they're all simply decorated and the same. What it lacks in character it makes up for in price, friendliness and its brilliant location. Good news for

families is that rooms are charged at a flat rate for up to three sharing. ☎ 454 0000 🖥 www .jurys.com ✉ Christ Church Pl 🖥 50, 54a, 56a, 150 🅿 ♿ ✕ Arches Restaurant 👶

La Stampa Hotel (6, D3) La Stampa is a wonderful, atmospheric little hotel on trendy Dawson St. It has 40 lovely Asian-influenced white rooms with Oriental rattan furniture, exotic velvet throws, TV, air conditioning and minibar. One considerable drawback for those travelling with all but the kitchen sink, is that bedrooms are up two flights of very steep stairs and there's no lift. Excellent value for its location. ☎ 677 4444 🖥 www .lastampa.ie ✉ 35 Dawson St 🖥 all cross-city

🚊 **St Stephen's Green** ✕ **La Stampa (p76)**

Number 31 (4, E9) Number 31 could be a set from the zeitgeist film *The Ice Storm*. The former home of modernist architect Sam Stephenson (of Central Bank fame) still feels like a real 1960s home, with its sunken sitting room, leather sofas, mirrored bar and Perspex lamps. Its 21 bedrooms are split between the retro coach house with its chichi rooms and the more gracious Georgian house, where rooms are individually furnished with French antiques and big beds. Gourmet breakfasts are served in the conservatory; children under 10 not permitted. ☎ 676 5011 🖥 www .number31.ie ✉ 31 Leeson Cl 🖥 11, 11a, 13b, 46, 58, 58c ✕

Escape to Dublin and the '60s at Number 31

Townhouse (4, E4) The Townhouse has all the hall-marks of a great guesthouse: 80 individually designed, comfy rooms with satellite TV, friendly and efficient staff, a city-centre location and a tab that won't burn a hole in your pocket. The colourful dining room leads out to a small Japanese garden. Highly recommended. ☎ 878 8808 ⬜ www .townhouseofdublin.com ✉ 47-48 Gardiner St Lower 🚌 Connolly Station 🚆 Abbey Street ✖ 101 Talbot (p68) ♿

BUDGET

Abbey Court Hostel (4, D5) Spread over two buildings on the Liffey quays, this large, well-run hostel has 33 clean dorms with good storage. En suite doubles with power showers are in the newer building, where a light breakfast is also provided in the adjacent café, Juice. ☎ 878 0700 ⬜ www .abbey-court.com ✉ 29 Bachelor's Walk 🚌 all cross-city 🚆 Abbey Street ♿ ✖ Juice (p73)

Barnacles Temple Bar House (5, C2) Bright and spacious, in the heart of Temple Bar, this hostel is immaculately clean, has nicely laid-out en suite dorms and doubles with that rare beast — in-room storage. Back rooms are quieter. Top facilities, comfy lounge, with linen and towels provided. ☎ 671 6277 ⬜ www .barnacles.ie ✉ 19 Tem-ple Lane 🚌 all cross-city ✖ ♿

Globetrotters Tourist Hostel (4, E4) This friendly, city-centre spot has 94 beds in a variety of en suite dorms, all with under-bed storage. Décor is funky and there's a little patio garden to the rear for the elusive sunny day. ☎ 878 8088 ⬜ gtrotter@ indigo.ie ✉ 46-48 Gar-diner St Lower 🚌 Con-nolly Station 🚆 Abbey Street ♿

Oliver St John Gogarty's Hostel (5, D2) Next door to the popular pub of the same name, this 124-bed hostel has bright, comfortable en suite dorms each with two to 10 beds. It tends to get booked up with stag and hen parties so, depending on your mood, bring your earplugs or bunny ears. Six self-catering apartments are also available. ☎ 671 1822 ⬜ www .gogartys.ie ✉ 18-21 Anglesea St 🚌 all cross-city ✖

Receptionist holding court at the Abbey Court Hostel

Gay Stays

Most of the city's hotels wouldn't bat an eyelid if same-sex couples checked in, but the same can't be said of many of the city's B&Bs. Exclusively gay places include:

Frankies Guesthouse (4, C8; ☎ 478 3087; www.frankiesguesthouse.com; 8 Camden Pl) Twelve homey rooms in an old mews house, with cable TV, full Irish breakfast and a plant-filled roof terrace.

Inn on the Liffey (4, B5; ☎ 677 0828; innontheliffey@hotmail.com; 21 Ormond Quay Upper) Compact and neat rooms on the northside quays, and guests have free access to the Dock sauna.

About Dublin

HISTORY
Early Inhabitants

The Celts, Iron Age warrior tribes from Eastern Europe, arrived in Dublin Bay around 700 BC, and adopted Christianity in the 5th century AD after St Patrick's mission to Ireland. Dublin's modern Irish name, Baile Átha Cliath, meaning 'Town of the Hurdle Ford', derives from an early Celtic settlement on the Liffey's northern bank.

Dublin became a major centre when Viking invaders established a trading port on the southern bank of the Liffey, near a *dubh linn* (black pool), in the early 9th century. In 1014 the Vikings were defeated by the Irish high king, Brian Ború, but it was the Normans, fresh from victory in England in 1066, who gained lasting control in the 12th century.

Medieval Dublin

Despite sustained growth, Dublin had a long run of bad luck during medieval times. In 1316 the Scots tried to invade, then in 1348 the Black Death devastated the population. Silken Thomas Fitzgerald launched a failed revolt against Henry VIII's garrison in Dublin in 1534. Three years later Henry dissolved the monasteries. But the establishment of Trinity College by Elizabeth I in 1592 ensured the city a shining educational tradition, albeit for future Protestants only.

Protestant Ascendancy

In 1649, Oliver Cromwell seized Dublin and cannily distributed Ireland's best land among his soldiers. Ireland backed Catholic James II in 1690's Battle of the Boyne, but when he was defeated by the Protestant

William of Orange, Catholics found themselves excluded from parliament and their every basic right denied by new penal laws. Drastically, expressions of Irish culture, music, language and religion were banned.

In the 18th century, the city boomed. The Protestant Huguenot weavers who fled from persecution in France established a successful cloth industry in the city. Trade flourished, and for a time Dublin was the fifth-largest city in Europe. But as the rich built fine Georgian mansions around stately squares, Dublin's largely Catholic poor lived in teeming slums.

Trinity College Long Room or bust

Dublin's Pale

The phrase 'beyond the pale' originated when Anglo-Norman control over Ireland was restricted to the narrow eastern coastal strip surrounding Dublin, known as the Pale. Outside this area – or 'Beyond the Pale' – Ireland remained a wild place, and fierce Irish warriors launched regular raids on English forces from their strongholds in the Wicklow mountains.

Disaster & Decline

The 19th century brought the human devastation of the Great Famine, attempted invasions, rebellions and unrest between Irish patriots and Britain. In 1801, England abolished the separate Irish Parliament. Failed revolts were launched by Wolfe Tone, Lord Edward Fitzgerald and later Robert Emmet. Daniel O'Connell had some success in his nonviolent campaign to recover basic rights for Catholics, but his political influence was limited.

While Dublin escaped the worst effects of the Potato Famine (1845–51), when the staple crop was blighted by disease, pitifully, its streets and squares became flooded with starving rural refugees.

Independence Struggles & Civil War

In 1882, the British chief secretary, Lord Cavendish, was assassinated in Phoenix Park (p28), and in 1905, Sinn Féin (We Ourselves), a republican political movement, was formed. But despite the ongoing struggles of a dedicated few, there was still little support for full Irish independence.

Another ill-planned revolt, the 1916 Easter Rising, laid waste to much of Dublin. But when the British executed the revolt's protagonists at

Kilmainham Gaol (p22) – including rebel leader Patrick Pearse – they succeeded in turning a band of rebels into martyrs, as well as consolidating a growing well of anti-British feeling.

After the Anglo–Irish War (1919–21) and months of negotiation, the Anglo–Irish Treaty was signed in 1921, creating the Irish Free State. It was not a full republic as the IRA had hoped for, but still subservient to Britain on many important issues. Nationalist rifts developed over the treaty, and fighting erupted between Free State supporters (led by Michael Collins) and anti-Treaty IRA forces (led by Sinn Féin president Eamon de Valera).

Historic Kilmainham Gaol

Divided We Fall

Dublin is split, physically and psychologically, by the river Liffey. Traditionally, areas north of the river have been poorer and more rundown, while the south boasts well-kept squares, expensive shops, restaurants and bars. But some Dubliners insist the real divide is east-west, with the wealthiest suburbs nearest the bay and the poorest suburbs to the west.

The 1960s and '70s saw major urban renewal and whole communities, who had spent generations in the inner city, uprooted and rehoused in new towns such as Ballymun and Darndale. The lucrative land was then rezoned for commercial use, but some say the heart and soul of the city was broken.

Did You Know?
- Dublin city traffic snarls are worse than those in New York, Tokyo and London. A study found it takes a car an average of 57 minutes to travel 5km
- Property prices have increased by more than 150% since 1990
- In 2001, 8000 people applied for asylum in Ireland; now the figure is just 350 per month
- The average Dubliner earns €26,000 a year, giving €15 to charity and €200 in tips
- Around 9800 pints of beer are drunk each hour by Dubliners from Friday night to Monday morning
- Women outnumber men in Dublin by 20,000

The Republic

Peace, of sorts, came in May 1923, when de Valera ordered the IRA to lay down its arms. In 1932, de Valera and his new party, Fianna Fáil, came to power, dropping all the treaty clauses they had fought against 10 years earlier. By WWII, Ireland – now called Éire – was a republic in all but name. Ireland left the British Commonwealth in 1949 and in 1955 became a member of the United Nations.

Universal free secondary education was introduced in the 1960s and the Republic joined the European Economic Community in 1973.

Dublin's economic climate changed dramatically in the 1990s, as interest rates tumbled, business burgeoned and foreign investment injected finance and reduced unemployment. But while the so-called Celtic Tiger economy is still much in evidence in the startling redevelopment of Dublin, not all sectors of society are benefiting. The true reflection of any nation can be seen in how it treats the marginalised. It still remains to be seen if the benefits of the Tiger economy have fully trickled down to those on the fringes of Dublin's society.

ENVIRONMENT

Though Dublin does not suffer the severe air pollution that chokes some other European cities, it has its share of environmental concerns. Worst among them is traffic congestion, which blights the city centre and particularly the Liffey quays.

On the positive side, the city is blessed with many parks, gardens and squares. Although recycling is slowly taking off, it is not yet part of the collective consciousness. Littering can be a problem, with cigarette butts and fast-food wrappers too often discarded on footpaths.

Good news for nonsmokers is that the days of coughing your way through a meal or pint is now a distant haze. As of March 2004 a smoking ban in public places was implemented and Dubliners (and visitors) will be all the healthier for it.

One solution to Dublin's traffic congestion

GOVERNMENT & POLITICS

The Republic of Ireland has a parliamentary system of government. Parliament's lower house, or house of representatives (Dáil Éireann, often shortened to Dáil), has 166 members elected by public ballot. Members of the upper house (Seanad) are nominated by the prime minister *(taoiseach)* or elected by university graduates and councillors. Both houses sit in Leinster House (p38) on Kildare St.

The president is the constitutional head of state, but has little real power.

The main political parties are Fianna Fáil, led by current prime minister Bertie Ahern, Fine Gael and the Labour Party. Of the remaining minor parties, Sinn Féin has the most support, garnering around 8% of the vote.

At local level, Dublin is governed by three elected bodies: Dublin City Council supervises the city; a county council looks after Dublin

Leinster House, the hub of Irish politics

County; and Dun Laoghaire & Rathdown Corporation administers the port town.

The current relatively popular government is a coalition of Fianna Fáil and the Progressive Democrats, in power since 1997.

ECONOMY

Ireland, and Dublin in particular, is in the throes (some say death throes) of its greatest period of economic success since independence. Signs of the so-called Celtic Tiger economy are everywhere and have prompted an explosion in tourism and a reversal of the age-old trend of emigration.

From 1993 to 1997 Ireland's economy grew by a whopping 40%, leading to record-low unemployment, higher standards of living and lower interest rates. But while growth continues today, it has levelled off significantly, and economists have expressed concern about rising inflation, interest rates and spiralling house prices.

Ireland's reliance on new technology and fickle foreign investment, however, is seen by some as the economy's vulnerable point.

SOCIETY & CULTURE

More than 50% of Dubliners are under 28 and almost a quarter are under 15 – a fact which goes a long way to explaining the city's vibrant, liberal outlook. While social stratification exists, years of British rule fostered a healthy contempt for snobbery and it is generally money, rather than breeding, which impresses here.

The population of Dublin is almost 1.2 million but the same again live within commuting distance of the centre. Although the city is predominantly Roman Catholic, the substantial Protestant minority has been boosted in recent years by immigrants from Africa and Eastern Europe. But the rapid growth in immigration has also exposed the raw nerves of racism in the city, with attacks and abuse all too common.

Ireland was the last country in Europe to legalise divorce, in a narrowly accepted 1995 referendum. While abortion remains illegal, women now have the right to unbiased information and to travel abroad for terminations. A ban on sex shops and the sale of contraceptives has also been lifted.

> **The Name Game**
> Visitors with Irish ancestry can try tracing their family tree at the National Library's **Genealogical Office** (6, F2; ☎ 603 0200; ☽ 10am-4.45pm Mon-Fri, to 12.30pm Sat). While the office won't do the work for you, it points you in the right direction, providing free information and expert advice.

Dos & Don'ts

Dublin is relaxed and easy-going, with few rigid rules and regulations. Probably the most important social tips for the visitor are those that apply to Irish pub culture.

The rounds system of buying a drink for all of your group is integral to pub life, and you'll quickly lose favour if you disrupt the balance.

In conversation, be aware that there is a marked difference between the views of the older and the younger generations. Young Dubliners are often extremely liberal, and sometimes radical, in their opinions, but older people might be reluctant to talk about issues such as sex, contraception, divorce or abortion. Religion and politics can also be volatile subjects, so tread carefully. Religious division, while an obvious point of difference in the north, is nonexistent in the Republic where the big divide is between those who are from Dublin and those who are not; those from the country are disparagingly referred to as 'culchies' – a byword for unsophisticates – by Dubliners. But it is a badge worn with pride by those from the country, who have an equally dismissive attitude towards Dubliners who they believe wrongly consider themselves superior.

Dubliners are generally relaxed and easy-going; unless you forget when it's your round

ARTS
Architecture

With Viking, Norman and medieval Dublin barely visible today, the neoclassical style of the Georgian era remains Dublin's most dominant architectural feature. During this period roads were widened, gardens and elegant squares laid out, the Liffey banked with concrete quays and a number of fine residences and public buildings constructed.

Many foreigners were drawn to the city during the Georgian period. The German Richard Cassels designed Powerscourt House (p50), Russborough House (p49), Newman House (p38) and Leinster House (p38). Englishman James Gandon's two riverside masterpieces, Custom House (p37) and the Four Courts (p37), remain two of Dublin's most enduring landmarks.

Buildings of note from the 20th century include: Busáras (4, E4), the International Modernist bus station designed by Michael Scott in the 1940s, and Paul Koralek's 1967 Berkeley Library (2, B2) at Trinity. The 1990s redevelopment of Temple Bar (p16) signalled the start of a major architectural renewal that continues to this day.

Literature

With their unique perspective on life, and their use of phrasing and expressions translated from Gaelic, Irish writers have made a phenomenal impact on English-language writing.

Jonathan Swift (1667–1745), the master satirist and author of *Gulliver's Travels*, was the greatest writer of the early Georgian period, closely followed by Oliver Goldsmith (1728–74, *The Vicar of Wakefield*) and poet

One of James Gandon's two riverside masterpieces, Custom House

> ## Bloomsday
> On 16 June each year, Joyce-lovers take to the streets in a re-enactment of Leopold Bloom's journey around Dublin in *Ulysses*. Various readings and dramatisations from Joyce's works take place around the city as folk in period costume, circa 1904, chow down on Gorgonzola cheese and glasses of Burgundy.
> Points of activity include the James Joyce Museum at Sandycove (p17) where *Ulysses* begins, Sweny's Chemist (2, D3), Davy Byrne's pub (2, A3) and the National Library (6, F2).

Thomas Moore (1779–1852). Oscar Wilde (1854–1900), renowned for his legendary wit, was educated at Trinity College but soon moved to London. The poet, playwright and statesman William Butler Yeats (1865–1939) won the Nobel Prize for literature in 1938 – an honour shared by fellow Dubliners George Bernard Shaw in 1925 and Samuel Beckett in 1969. Bram Stoker (1847–1912), the creator of Dracula, also hailed from this fair city.

James Joyce is the city's most famous literary son. References to his great Dublin novel *Ulysses* can be found all over the city and the book is the inspiration for annual Bloomsday celebrations (above).

In more recent times Dublin schoolteacher Roddy Doyle *(The Commitments)* has had much success, including winning the Booker Prize in 1993 for *Paddy Clarke, Ha Ha Ha*. John Banville also bagged the Booker for *Book of Evidence* in 1989. Brendan Behan, Patrick McCabe, Flann O'Brien, Liam O'Flaherty and Sean O'Faolain are other Irish writers of note, while young scribblers to look out for include Pat Boran, Philip McCann, Emer Martin and Emma Donoghue.

He of the Wilde wit at Merrion Sq

Music
From traditional music through to rock and pop, tiny Ireland has been disproportionately represented on the world stage. Perhaps the best known traditional Gaelic music group is the Chieftains. Other notables include Scullion, the Wolfe Tones and the Fureys. Though more a folk band than a traditional outfit, the Dubliners have been around for more than 30 years.

The godfather of Irish singer-songwriters is Christy Moore, who is hugely popular for his folk-style music. Appealing to younger audiences, Paddy Casey has been compared to David Gray for his melodic arrangements and intelligent lyrics. Songwriter Mark Geary, returned from New York, has been wowing audiences with his bittersweet tunes. Soul-folk-rockers the Frames have a phenomenally loyal following and are highly rated for their live performances.

Boy-next-door Daniel O'Donnell is a favourite with the over-40s. Female singers like Mary and Frances Black, Mary Coughlan and Eleanor McEvoy are now being challenged by new stars including Juliet Turner, Nina Hynes and Gemma Hayes.

Belfast-born Van Morrison put Ireland on the world rock map in the 1960s, followed by the likes of Thin Lizzy and the Boomtown Rats in the 1970s and '80s. The Cranberries, from Limerick, and the Corrs, from Dundalk, emerged more recently, as did the controversial Sinéad O'Connor. But none have achieved the phenomenal success of U2, the megastar Dublin band that has been churning out hits for more than 20 years.

In the 'treacle-pop' category, Boyzone had thousands of 12-year-olds in tears when they split in 2000, but Westlife quickly filled the void with their big smiles and dance routines.

Credible rock bands to watch out for are Snow Patrol, the Thrills and Future Kings of Spain.

Theatre

Dublin's theatrical history is almost as long as its literary one. The city's first theatre was founded in Werburgh St in 1637, though it was closed by the Puritans four years later. Today the city's most famous playhouse, and Ireland's National Theatre, is the Abbey (p91), established in 1904 by WB Yeats and Lady Gregory.

After years in the doldrums following the successes of famous playwrights Wilde, Yeats, Shaw and Beckett, Irish theatre is undergoing something of a renaissance. A number of new companies are staging thought-provoking, contemporary plays as well as new spins on old classics. Look out for the likes of Rough Magic, Pig's Back and Cornmarket, as well as playwrights Conor McPherson, Martin McDonagh and Mark O'Rowe.

'I loved it', 'I hated it', 'I loved it'... the masks are divided over the Gaiety Theatre's latest

Directory

Travellers sit back and reflect on their time in Dublin at St Stephen's Green

ARRIVAL & DEPARTURE
Air

Dublin airport (1, C1; www.dublin-airport.com) is 13km north of the city centre and has an exchange bureau, post office and Dublin Tourism office.

INFORMATION

General Inquiries	☎ 814 1111
Car Park Information	☎ 814 4328

Flight Information:

Aer Lingus	☎ 886 6705
British Midland	☎ 814 4259
City Jet	☎ 844 5577
Ryanair	☎ 1550 200 200

AIRPORT ACCESS
Airlink Express

Operated by **Dublin Bus** (☎ 872 0000; www.dublinbus.ie), Airlink Express runs two buses between the airport and city centre at a flat rate of €5: No 747, to/from Busáras (4, E4), the central bus station, and the Dublin Bus office (4, D4) on O'Connell St; and No 748, to/from Heuston Station (3, D3) and Connolly Station (4, F3). The trip takes 30 to 40 minutes or more.

Aircoach

Luxury **Aircoach** (☎ 844 7118; www.aircoach.ie; ☻ 5am-11.30pm) buses operate between the airport and 15 locations in Dublin. Stops include: Gresham Hotel (4, D3), corner of Trinity College and Grafton St (2, A2), Merrion Sq (4, F7), Leeson St (4, E8) and Dawson St (6, E2). Another goes to the International Financial Services Centre (4, F4) and Connolly Station (4, F3) before going north to Malahide (1, C1). One-way trips cost €6.

Public Bus

Nos 41, 41a and 41c go to Eden Quay (4, D5) near O'Connell St.

The often-crowded journey can take over an hour, but at €1.65 it's cheap.

Taxi

A taxi to the centre takes about half an hour and costs around €20. There's a supplementary charge of €1 from the airport and additional charges for baggage.

Boat

Ferry services from Britain sail to two ports in Dublin. The **Dublin city ferry terminal** (☎ 855 2222) is 3km east of the centre and public transport is linked to departures and arrivals. The **Carlisle ferry terminal** (☎ 280 1905), at Dun Laoghaire (1, C1) on the southern side of Dublin Bay, is easily accessible by DART or public bus.

From the UK, **Stena Line** (UK ☎ 0990 707 070, Dun Laoghaire 204 7600; www.stenaline.co.uk) operates speedy services for passengers and cars from Holyhead in Wales to Dun Laoghaire (1½ hours) and a car-only ferry from Holyhead to Dublin (3½ hours). **Irish Ferries** (UK ☎ 0990 171 717, Dublin 1890 313 131; www.irishferries.com; 2-4 Merrion Row) operates passenger and car ferries from Holyhead to Dublin.

Bus

Busáras (4, E4; Store St) is Dublin's central bus station and plays host to **Bus Éireann** (☎ 836 6111; www.buseireann.ie), the Republic's national bus line. Private bus companies that run services around the country include **Nestor Coaches** (☎ 832 0094) to Galway, and **JJ Kavanagh Rapid Express** (☎ 679 1549; www.jjkavanagh.ie) to Waterford and Limerick.

Bus Éireann and, from the UK, **National Express** (UK ☎ 0870 580 8080; www .national express.com) also operate the **Eurolines services** (www.eurolines.com) direct from

London and other UK centres to Dublin.

Irish Rambler tickets (three-/eight-/15-day ticket €53/116/168) are available from Bus Éireann and allow unlimited bus travel within the Republic.

Train

Although the train network is improving, it is still slow, expensive and poorly maintained. **Iarnród Éireann** (Irish Rail; 4, D4; ☎ 836 6222; www.irishrail.ie; 35 Abbey St Lower) operates the Republic's trains on routes that fan out from Dublin.

Connolly Station (4, F3; ☎ 836 3333) has trains to Belfast, Derry and other points in the north. **Heuston Station** (3, D3; ☎ 836 5421) has services to Cork, Galway, Limerick and other points throughout the Republic.

The Emerald Card (eight days' travel over 15 days/15 days' travel over 30 days €198/340) offers you unlimited train and bus travel on several carriers throughout the Republic and Northern Ireland.

Travel Documents
PASSPORT

Passports are not required by UK-born British citizens travelling from Britain, but bring some ID. EU citizens may use a passport or national ID card. All other nationalities must carry a valid passport.

VISA

EU citizens can stay indefinitely and nationals of Australia, Canada, Japan, New Zealand, South Africa and the USA need no visa if entering as a tourist for up to three months.

RETURN/ONWARD TICKET

A return or onward ticket may be required if there's any doubt that you have sufficient funds to support yourself in Ireland.

Customs & Duty Free

The import and export of currency is unrestricted. Goods brought in and exported within the EU incur no additional taxes, provided duty has been paid in the EU and goods are for personal consumption.

Duty-free sales within the EU no longer exist. For those travelling between Ireland and a non-EU country, the duty-free limits are: 200 cigarettes, 2L of wine, 1L of spirits or strong liquor (over 22% alcohol), 60mL of perfume, and 250mL of eau de toilette.

Left Luggage

Busáras (4, E4; ☎ 836 6111; €4-9 per locker; ☽ 7am-10.45pm), the main bus depot.

Connolly Station (4, F3; ☎ 836 6222; €2.50 per bag; ☽ 7am-10pm Mon-Sat, from 8am Sun).

Greencaps Left Luggage & Porterage Office (☎ 814 4633; €4-8 per item for 24hr; ☽ 6am-11pm), in the car park in Dublin airport (1, C1).

Heuston Station (3, D3; ☎ 836 6222; €1.50-5 per locker for 24hr; ☽ 7am-10pm Mon-Sat, from 8am Sun).

GETTING AROUND

Dublin's buses and train service do little to ease the appalling street congestion. Getting around the centre is best done on foot or bicycle and trips further out should be timed to avoid rush hours. The long-awaited LUAS light-rail service finally arrived in June 2004.

In this book the DART/bus/light rail-stations are noted after the 🚊 / 🚌 / 🚃 symbol in each listing.

Travel Passes

Rambler bus passes are available for one/three/five/seven days for €5/10/15/18. A one-day family Rambler is excellent value.

Rail-only passes, for DART and suburban train services, cost €20.60/76 for a week/month. An adult pass combining rail and bus costs €15/26 for use on three/seven consecutive days (ID photo required).

Bus passes should be bought in advance from Dublin Bus (below) or from the many ticket agents around the city (look for signs in shop windows). Buy rail passes from any DART or suburban rail stations or the Iarnród Éireann (p113) office.

Bus

Dublin Bus (4, D4; ☎ 873 4222; www.dublinbus.ie; 59 O'Connell St Upper; ◷ 9am-5.30pm Mon-Fri, to 2pm Sat) has buses that are usually blue-and-cream double-deckers or small, red-and-yellow ones called 'Imps'. They run from 6am to 11.30pm, less frequently on Sundays. Fares are calculated on stages travelled, from €0.85 for up to three stages to €1.65 for up to 23. Tender exact change when boarding; if you pay too much a receipt is issued, which is reimbursed at the Dublin Bus office.

Dublin bus also runs Nitelink buses on 22 routes at 12.30am and 2am Monday to Saturday nights, usually with extra services every 20 minutes from 12.30am to 4.30am on Friday and Saturday nights. Buses depart from the area around College St, Westmoreland St and D'Olier St (4, D5). Most journeys cost €4.

Train

Dublin Area Rapid Transport (DART) runs along the coast as far north as Howth (1, C1) and Malahide (1, C1) and as far south as Bray (1, C2). Services depart every 10 to 20 minutes, from 6.30am to midnight, and less frequently on Sundays.

One-way tickets from central Dublin to Dun Laoghaire (1, C1)/

Howth cost €1.80; to Bray it's €2.10. A one-day unlimited DART ticket costs €6.50.

Light Rail

Dublin's new light-rail system (LUAS) runs one line from Sandyford north to St Stephen's Green (4, D7) and one line from Tallaght east via Heuston Station (3, D3) into Abbey St (4, D4) in the city centre. A short line from Abbey St to Connolly Station (4, F3) is also under construction. Trains run from 5.30am to 12.30am every 15 minutes and every five minutes during morning and evening peak times. Tickets are available from machines at stops and certain newsagents.

Taxi

Taxis can be hailed on the street or found at ranks, including those at O'Connell St (4, D3), College Green (2, A1) and St Stephen's Green N (6, D3) near Grafton St.

It can be difficult to get a taxi after pubs close Thursday to Saturday. Many companies dispatch taxis by radio but run out of cars at peak times; be sure to book as early as you can. Try **City Cabs** (☎ 872 7272) or **National Radio Cabs** (☎ 677 2222).

Flagfall is €2.75, then €0.15 for every ⅑ mile (or 30 seconds); supplements include phone bookings (€1.50), night travel (€0.50) and luggage (€0.50 per item).

Car & Motorcycle

On a short trip to Dublin you're unlikely to need your own wheels, besides which the traffic congestion, scarce parking and extremely diligent clampers will not make driving here a pleasant experience.

Secure car parks are recommended by the police, but they can be expensive. Unleaded petrol costs about €0.90 per L with diesel a bit less.

ROAD RULES
Driving is on the left. It's obligatory for all passengers to wear a seatbelt and children under 12 are not allowed in front seats.

RENTAL
Dublin's car rental firms include **Avis** (☎ 605 7555; www.avis.com), **Argus** (☎ 490 4444; www.argus-rentacar.com) and **Budget** (☎ 837 9802; www.budgetcarrental.ie). Typical high-season rates start at €45/240 per day/week.

PRACTICALITIES
Climate & When to Go
Dublin's peak tourist period is July and August when the weather is warmest and days longest, but expect big crowds at sights, higher costs and scarce accommodation. In quieter winter months weather is usually miserable, days shorter and some tourist facilities shut. June or September is best: weather is pleasant and it's less crowded. Visiting around St Patrick's Day (March 17) is recommended as the city celebrates with a parade, fireworks, street dancing and other events.

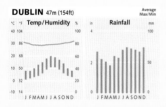

Disabled Travellers
Guesthouses, hotels and sights in Ireland are slowly being adapted for people with disabilities, but there is still a long way to go. A great deal of sights, hotels and shops are located in historic buildings that have no disabled access and cannot have lifts or ramps installed because of preservation orders.

Public transport is also problematic; some buses have low floors and designated wheelchair spots, many do not. For train travel, call ahead for an employee of Iarnród Éireann (Irish Rail; p113) to accompany you to the train and to help you off at your destination.

Wheelchair-accessible venues listed in this book appear with a ♿ symbol followed by the description 'excellent' (wheelchair access throughout the venue), 'good' (some access) and 'limited' (limited access). If in doubt, call ahead to check.

INFORMATION & ORGANISATIONS
Fáilte Ireland's annual accommodation guide, *Be Our Guest,* is available from Fáilte Ireland's larger offices and lists places that are wheelchair accessible. Obtain general information from **Comhairle** (☎ 874 7503).

Other useful organisations include:

Catholic Institute for the Deaf
 ☎ 830 0522

Enable Ireland (Cerebral Palsy Ireland)
 ☎ 269 5355

Cystic Fibrosis Association of Ireland
 ☎ 496 2433

Irish Wheelchair Association
 ☎ 661 6183

Discounts
Most of Dublin's attractions offer discounts to children under 16, students and the elderly. Family tickets usually give entry to two adults and two children.

Heritage Cards (p8) give unlimited admission for one year to sites managed by the Office of Public Works in Ireland.

STUDENT & YOUTH CARDS
The International Student Identity Card (ISIC) is accepted at sights and on public transport.

The **An Óige** (Irish Youth Hostel Association; 4, C2; ☎ 830 4555; 61 Mountjoy St) sells a card for €20 that offers hostel discounts.

SENIORS' CARDS
Senior citizens usually need only show proof of age to receive discounts, including government and privately run sights and on public transport.

Electricity

Voltage	220V
Frequency	50Hz
Cycle	AC
Plugs	flat three-pin type

Embassies
Australia (4, F9; ☎ 676 1517; 2nd fl, Fitzwilton House, Wilton Tce)

Canada (4, D8; ☎ 478 1988; 4th fl, 65-68 St Stephen's Green)

South Africa (4, D9; ☎ 661 5553; Earlsfort Centre, Earlsfort Tce)

UK (3, J6; ☎ 205 3700; 29 Merrion Rd)

USA (3, H5; ☎ 668 8777; 42 Elgin Rd)

Emergencies
Dublin is one of Europe's safest capitals, but pickpocketing and car break-ins are on the rise. Increased immigration has stirred racial harassment. Though thankfully infrequent, report serious incidents to police.

Ambulance, Fire, Police	☎ 999, 112
Police (non-emergency)	☎ 666 6666
Rape Crisis Line	☎ 1800 778 888

Gay & Lesbian Travellers
For such an overwhelmingly Catholic country, Irish laws on homosexuality are surprisingly progressive. In Dublin the gay and lesbian scene is loud, proud and very vibrant. It is most obvious in the city centre, with several gay bars and clubs around Temple Bar and another batch of bars and saunas on the northside around Ormond Quay. There are even a couple of specialist gay B&Bs (p102).

INFORMATION & ORGANISATIONS
Gay Community News (www .gcn.ie) is a free publication available at various cafés and bars in town.

Gay Switchboard (☎ 872 1055; ☿ 8-10pm Sun-Fri, 3.30-6pm Sat)

Lesbian Line (☎ 872 9911; ☿ 7-9pm Thu)

Outhouse (☎ 873 4932; www.out house.ie) is the national Lesbian & Gay Federation.

Health
IMMUNISATIONS
No vaccinations are required to enter Ireland.

PRECAUTIONS
Dublin has no serious health problems. Although Ireland is still a largely rural country, there is no risk of contracting rabies due to stringent laws banning importation of any animal products. Tap water is safe to drink and be prepared for lots of rain, even in summer.

MEDICAL SERVICES
Travel insurance is advisable to cover medical treatment you may need while in Dublin. The **Eastern Regional Health Authority** (☎ 635 2000, 1800 520 520; www .erha.ie), which is housed in **Dr Steevens' Hospital** (3, D3), has a Choice of Doctor Scheme, which can advise you on suitable doctors 9am to 5pm Monday to Friday. Your hotel can also suggest a doctor.

Several countries have reciprocal agreements with Ireland for treatment of visitors. EU citizens are entitled to free hospital treatment and should obtain an E111 form prior to departure.

Hospitals with 24-hour accident and emergency departments include **Mater Misericordiae Hospital** (4, B1; ☎ 803 2000; Eccles St) and **St James's Hospital** (3, D4; ☎ 453 7941; James St).

DENTAL SERVICES

If you're unfortunate enough to chip a tooth or require emergency treatment, head to the **Dental Hospital** (2, D3; ☎ 612 7200; 20 Lincoln Pl; ☯ 8am or noon for same-day appointments).

PHARMACIES

The following pharmacies are open late:

Dame St Pharmacy (5, B3; ☎ 670 4523; 16 Dame St; ☯ 8am-10pm)

O'Connell's Late -Night Pharmacy (4, D5; ☎ 873 0427; 55 O'Connell St Lower; ☯ 7.30am-10pm)

Holidays

Jan 1	New Year's Day
Mar 17	St Patrick's Day
Mar/Apr	Good Friday
Mar/Apr	Easter Monday
May 1	May Day
Jun	June Holiday (first Mon)
Aug	August Holiday (first Mon)
Oct	October Holiday (last Mon)
Dec 25	Christmas Day
Dec 26	St Stephen's Day

Internet

Internet cafés are dotted all over the city, and many of then are open until late. Most public libraries offer an Internet service, usually for little or no cost. If you've packed your laptop, note that the Republic uses a square-pinned, three-pronged power plug and most hotel fittings take RJ-11 phone jacks.

INTERNET SERVICE PROVIDERS

Most of the major global Internet Service Providers (ISPs) have dial-in nodes available in Ireland; it's a good idea to download lists of the dial-in numbers before you leave home.

If you access the Internet through one of the smaller ISPs, your best option is to open an account with a global ISP or sign on to a local provider while in Ireland.

In Dublin, local ISPs include Eircom.net, Oceanfree and IOL, who offer a nonsubscription-based service with timed usage charged on a metered phone line.

INTERNET CAFÉS

Does Not Compute (4, C6; ☎ 670 4464; Unit 2, Pudding Row, Essex St W; ☯ 9am-11pm) also at Bleeding Horse pub (4, C9; ☎ 4766 4928; 25 Camden St Upper)

Global Internet Café Basement (4, D4; ☎ 878 0295; 8 O'Connell St Lower; ☯ 8am-11pm Mon-Fri, from 9am Sat, from 10am Sun)

Internet Exchange (5, C2; ☎ 670 3000; 3 Cecilia St; ☯ 8-2am Mon-Fri, 10am-midnight Sat & Sun)

USEFUL WEBSITES

The Lonely Planet website (www .lonelyplanet.com) offers a convenient and speedy link to many of Dublin's websites.

Others websites worth a browse include:

Dublin Tourism
www.visitdublin.com

Fáilte Ireland
www.ireland.travel.ie

Irish Times
www.ireland.com

World's Best Bars
www.worldsbestbars.com

Lost Property

Report all lost property to police to validate insurance claims. To retrieve lost items call:

Bus Éireann	☎ 703 2489
Dublin Airport	☎ 814 4483
Dublin Bus	☎ 703 1321
Connolly Station	☎ 703 2363
Ferry Services	☎ 855 2296
Heuston Station	☎ 703 2102
Taxis Carriage Office	☎ 475 5888

Metric System

Ireland uses the metric system but imperial measurements are still common. Speed limits are in miles, food may be weighed in either kilograms or pounds and beer comes in pints.

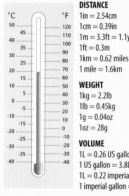

TEMPERATURE
°C = (°F - 32) ÷ 1.8
°F = (°C x 1.8) + 32

DISTANCE
1in = 2.54cm
1cm = 0.39in
1m = 3.3ft = 1.1yd
1ft = 0.3m
1km = 0.62 miles
1 mile = 1.6km

WEIGHT
1kg = 2.2lb
1lb = 0.45kg
1g = 0.04oz
1oz = 28g

VOLUME
1L = 0.26 US gallons
1 US gallon = 3.8L
1L = 0.22 imperial gallons
1 imperial gallon = 4.55L

Money
CURRENCY

In 2002, as part of the European Union (EU), Ireland adopted the European single currency, the euro. The euro is divided into 100 cents (c). Coins come in 1c, 2c, 5c, 10c, 20c and 50c, as well as €1 and €2. Note denominations are €5, €10, €20, €50, €100, €200 and €500.

TRAVELLERS CHEQUES

Most major brands of travellers cheques are accepted in Ireland and can be cashed at exchange offices, banks and some post offices. Try **Thomas Cook** (6, D3; ☎ 677 1721; 118 Grafton St) or **American Express** (2, A2; ☎ 679 9000; 41 Nassau St). Travellers cheques are rarely accepted for everyday transactions so be sure to cash them beforehand.

CREDIT CARDS

Major credit cards, especially American Express, MasterCard and Visa, are widely accepted, though some B&Bs only take cash. For 24-hour card cancellations or assistance call:

American Express	☎ 1800 282 728
Diners Club	☎ 1800 409 204
MasterCard	☎ 1800 557 378
Visa	☎ 1800 558 002

ATMS

Irish ATMs are linked up to international systems such as Cirrus, Maestro or Plus. The Allied Irish Bank (AIB) and Bank of Ireland have many centrally located ATMs.

CHANGING MONEY

Banks usually have the best exchange rates and lowest commission charges, though money-changers open later. Many post offices have currency exchange counters. There's a cluster of banks in College Green (2, A2), opposite Trinity College, all with exchange facilities.

Newspapers & Magazines

The main Irish dailies are the *Irish Times* (www.ireland.com), *Irish Independent* (www.unison.ie) and *Irish Examiner* (www.irish examiner.ie). The *Evening Herald* is an evening tabloid, while Sunday papers include the *Sunday Tribune* and the *Sunday Business Post*, the best financial newspaper in the country. The free *Dublin Event Guide* is the main entertainment-listings magazine.

British papers and magazines are available on the day of issue and are cheaper than Irish papers. **Eason's** (4, D4; ☎ 837 3811; 40 O'Connell St Lower) and other large newsagents sell wide selections of foreign and regional Irish papers.

Opening Hours

Banks
10am-4pm Mon-Fri, to 5pm Thu

Offices
9am-5pm Mon-Fri

Post Offices
8.30am-5.30pm or 6pm Mon-Fri, 9am-1pm Sat. *GPO* 8am-8pm Mon-Sat

Shops
Most open 9am or 10am-6pm Mon-Sat, to 8pm Thu; noon-6pm Sun

Photography & Video
Print and slide film, camera gear and repairs are readily available from the many camera shops in the centre.

Developing and printing a 24-exposure print film typically costs around €12 for a one-hour service or from €6.50 for a slower turnaround. Slide processing costs about €10 a roll.

Ireland uses the VHF PAL system for video, which is incompatible with NTSC or SECAM.

Post
An Post (the Irish Postal Service) is reliable, efficient and usually on time. Aside from the **GPO** (4, D4; O'Connell St Lower), the post offices on Anne St S (6, D2) and St Andrew's St (5, D3) are close to the centre. Some newsagents operate as sub-post offices, and most sell stamps.

POSTAL RATES

Destination	Cost
Up to 25g	
Ireland	48c
Britain	60c
Rest of world	65c
Up to 50g	
Ireland	60c
Britain	90c
Rest of world	€1.20

Radio
Radio na Telefís Éireann (RTE) is Ireland's state broadcasting body. There are three state-controlled radio stations. Two – RTE's Radio 1 (89.6FM) and 2FM (91.8FM) – are broadcast in English, and Radio na Gaeltachta (92–93FM) in Irish. Commercial stations include: 98FM, 104FM, Q102 (102FM) and Today FM (100.2FM).

Telephone
Local calls from a public phone cost €0.25 for three minutes. Eircom is Ireland's largest service provider, and all of Dublin's public phones bear its name. Public phones accept coins, phonecards and/or credit cards or reverse charges.

The cheapest place for international calls in Dublin is at **Talk Shop** (www.talkshop.ie), with several branches across the city centre, including the Granary, (5, C2; ☎ 672 7212; 20 Temple Lane S; 🕙 9am-11pm) and north of the Liffey (4, D4; ☎ 872 0200; 5 O'Connell St Upper; 🕙 9am-11pm).

PHONECARDS
Prepaid phonecards (known as callcards) are widely available from newsagents and post offices. They come in units of 10, 20 and 50. One unit equals a local phone call.

Lonely Planet also has a competitively priced phonecard and a range of other travel services, all on offer at www.lonelyplanet.com /travel_services.

MOBILE PHONES

Ireland uses the GSM 900/1800 cellular phone system, which is compatible with European and Australian, but not North American or Japanese, phones.

There are four Irish service providers: Eircell (087), Vodafone (087), O2 (086) and Meteor (085). All have links with most international GSM providers, which allow you to 'roam' onto a local service on arrival. You can also purchase a pay-as-you-go package with a local provider with your own mobile phone.

COUNTRY & CITY CODES

Ireland	☎ 353
Dublin	☎ 01

USEFUL PHONE NUMBERS

Directory Inquiries	☎ 11811
International Directory Inquiries	☎ 11818
International Operator	☎ 114
Ireland/Great Britain Operator	☎ 10
Time	☎ 1191
Weather	☎ 1550 123822

INTERNATIONAL DIRECT DIAL CODES

Dial ☎ 00 followed by:

Australia	☎ 61
Canada	☎ 1
Japan	☎ 81
South Africa	☎ 27
UK	☎ 44
USA	☎ 1

Television

Ireland has three state-controlled TV channels: RTE 1, Network 2 and the Irish-language TnaG. There's also an independent station, TV3. British BBC1 and BBC2, ITV and Channel 4 programmes can also be picked up. Satellite TV channels include Sky, MTV and UK Gold.

Time

Dublin Standard Time is on GMT/ UTC. Daylight-saving time is practised mid-March to late October. At noon in Dublin it's:

7am in New York

3am in Los Angeles

noon in London

2pm in Johannesburg

10pm in Sydney

Tipping

Tipping is becoming more common, but is still not as prevalent as in the USA or the rest of Europe. If a restaurant adds a service charge (usually 10%) no tip is required. If not, most people tip 10% and round up taxi fares. For hotel porters €1 per bag is acceptable.

Tourist Information

Information on Dublin and all of Ireland is available from the national tourist office, Fáilte Ireland (www.ireland.travel.ie).

The main tourist authority is Dublin Tourism, with three walk-in only city-centre services. The **Dublin Tourism Centre** (5, D3; ☎ 605 7700; www.visitdublin.ie; 2 Suffolk St; ☺ 8.30am-6.30pm Mon-Sat, 10.30am-3.30pm Sun Jul & Aug; 9am-5.30pm Mon-Sat Sep-Jun), is by far the biggest. As well as being a great source of information, the centre can book accommodation and tours. The other Dublin Tourism branches are at 14 O'Connell St (4, D4) and at the Baggot St Bridge, in the foyer of **Fáilte Ireland** (3, G4; ☎ 1 850 230 330).

Dublin Tourism phone reservations are provided by Gulliver Info Res, a computerised service that provides up-to-date information on events, attractions and transport as well as booking accommodation. In Ireland call ☎ 1 800 668 668; in Britain ☎ 0800 668 668 66; from the rest of the world ☎ 353 669 792 083.

Women Travellers

In Dublin women are treated in the same way as in any cosmopolitan city. Obviously, lone women should exercise caution when walking at night or in dodgy areas.

Oral contraceptives are available with a doctor's prescription, and tampons are widely available at chemists or supermarkets. The

Well Woman Centre (3, G5; ☎ 660 9860; www.wellwomancentre.ie; 67 Pembroke Rd) advises on women's health issues and can prescribe the morning-after pill. It has another centre on Leeson St Lower (4, E8).

LANGUAGE

English is spoken in Dublin, although the national language, Irish (a Gaelic language), is more commonly spoken in parts of rural Ireland. All official documents and street signs are in Irish or bilingual.

Dubliners' style of English, particularly the inventive vocabulary, has been lauded throughout the English-speaking world. The syntax used by Dubliners – and the Irish in general – involves a unique word order that is usually related to the Irish language.

Index

See also separate indexes for Eating (p125), Sleeping (p126), Shopping (p125) and Sights with map references (p127).

SHOPPING

EATING

SLEEPING

Sight Index

FEATURES

[Epicurean Food Stall]	*Eating*
[Savoy]	*Entertainment*
[Bailey]	*Drinking*
[Bang Café]	*Café*
[Guinness Store House]	*Highlights*
[Smyths Toys)]	*Shopping*
[National Library]	*Sights/Activities*
[La Stampa Hotel]	*Sleeping*

AREAS

- Beach, Desert
- Building
- Land
- Mall
- Other Area
- Park/Cemetary
- Sports
- Urban

HYDROGRAPHY

- River, Creek
- Intermittent River
- Canal
- Swamp
- Water

BOUNDARIES

- State, Provincial
- Regional, Suburb
- Ancient Wall

ROUTES

- Tollway
- Freeway
- Primary Road
- Secondary Road
- Tertiary Road
- Lane
- Under Construction
- One-Way Street
- Unsealed Road
- Mall/Steps
- Tunnel
- Walking Path
- Walking Trail
- Track
- Walking Tour

TRANSPORT

- Airport, Airfield
- Bus Route
- Cycling, Bicycle Path
- Ferry
- General Transport
- Metro
- Monorail
- Rail
- Taxi Rank
- Tram

SYMBOLS

- Bank, ATM
- Buddhist
- Castle, Fortress
- Christian
- Diving, Snorkeling
- Embassy, Consulate
- Hospital, Clinic
- Information
- Internet Access
- Islamic
- Jewish
- Lighthouse
- Lookout
- Monument
- Mountain, Volcano
- National Park
- Parking Area
- Petrol Station
- Picnic Area
- Point of Interest
- Police Station
- Post Office
- Ruin
- Telephone
- Toilets
- Zoo, Bird Sanctuary
- Waterfall

24/7 travel advice
www.lonelyplanet.com